Freud's Beasty Boys

Freud's Beasty Boys

Sex, Violence and Masculinity

Oxana Timofeeva

polity

Copyright © MSB Matthes & Seitz Berlin Verlagsgesellschaft mbH, Berlin 2025. All rights reserved.

First published by Polity Press in 2025

Polity Press
65 Bridge Street
Cambridge CB2 1UR, UK

Polity Press
111 River Street
Hoboken, NJ 07030, USA

All rights reserved. Except for the quotation of short passages for the purpose of criticism and review, no part of this publication may be reproduced, stored in a retrieval system or transmitted, in any form or by any means, electronic, mechanical, photocopying, recording or otherwise, without the prior permission of the publisher.

ISBN-13: 978-1-5095-6840-6
ISBN-13: 978-1-5095-6841-3(pb)

A catalogue record for this book is available from the British Library.

Library of Congress Control Number: 2024943753

Typeset in 11 on 13pt Sabon
by Cheshire Typesetting Ltd, Cuddington, Cheshire
Printed and bound in Great Britain by CPI Group (UK) Ltd, Croydon

The publisher has used its best endeavours to ensure that the URLs for external websites referred to in this book are correct and active at the time of going to press. However, the publisher has no responsibility for the websites and can make no guarantee that a site will remain live or that the content is or will remain appropriate.

Every effort has been made to trace all copyright holders, but if any have been overlooked the publisher will be pleased to include any necessary credits in any subsequent reprint or edition.

For further information on Polity, visit our website:
politybooks.com

Contents

Acknowledgments	vi
Introduction	1
1 The Theater of the Soul	6
2 A Horse Is Being Beaten	21
3 A Rathole	50
4 The Number of Beasts	71
Notes	99
Bibliography	108
Index	113

Acknowledgments

I thank those without whom I would not have written this book: my teacher, Valery Podoroga (1946–2020), who gave me my first insight into Freud in Moscow in 1999; my adviser at the Jan van Eyck Academy in Maastricht, Katja Dieffenbach, who encouraged me to think about the number of beasts in 2010–11, the troika of philosophers from Ljubljana – Slavoj Žižek, Mladen Dolar, and Alenka Zupančič – who showed how to reconcile philosophy and psychoanalysis, and my friend Elena Kostyleva, who knows how many wolves there are. I also thank the Alexander von Humboldt Foundation for granting me a fellowship, which allowed me to stay in Berlin for the seven months it took to complete this book in 2023, and Susanne Frank for being my host at Humboldt University for this research period. Finally, my gratitude is to those who were present to help and encourage me to keep on going: my family, friends, and animals (including the three hedgehogs that live under the porch of my cottage).

Introduction

The theme of this book is violence and sexuality after Freud. Its characters, though, are not women or men, but animals and children. It mainly focuses on three famous Freudian psychoanalytical cases where animals are at stake – Little Hans, the Rat Man, and the Wolf Man – and revises the role played by animals in male gender socialization. I assume that beyond sexuality, which, according to Freud, creates the background of our psychic lives, there is a mechanism of violence implemented in the production of a social norm as we know it. I call it the machine of masculinity, but do not insist on this term – you can call it something else. It is a dynamic configuration that can be approached on different levels – psychological, anthropological, theological, or metaphysical. Without claiming to describe it exhaustively, I am trying to understand how it functions – either with Freud, or against him – using a few examples.

Some people think that Freud is outdated and that anyone who wants to understand modernity has to address more recent authors. Perhaps from the point of view of clinical psychology such statements make sense, but in philosophy no one ever becomes obsolete: although Freud was not a

Introduction

philosopher in the strict sense, his work opens up a speculative horizon that extends to infinity. Only prejudices can prevent us from returning to his cases and applying the elements of his analysis to our own cases today, to stories and situations of varying degrees of insanity.

However, this is not a scholarly work dedicated to a single author, but rather a somewhat elusive and divergent exercise in reflection, which I have been doing on and off over the past few years. With regard to Freud's discussions about girls with sexual fantasies or boys with animal phobias, I outline the contours of a very preliminary and far from systematic account, but still my own version of philosophical anthropology as it relates to the analysis (and self-analysis) of the human soul. The word "human" is, of course, conventional, and is used here only for the purpose of inviting everyone to apply such analysis to themselves. I do by no means intend to say that there is such a thing as a human soul different from the psyche of any other being. It would be better to speak of an animal soul – the self-analysis of our animal soul – not in itself, but in the context of Western culture with its particular scenarios of psychic drama played out over and over again at the intersection of fantasy and reality.

Up until 2023, I did not know that I was working on this book, but was simply addressing psychoanalysis with some philosophical questions from time to time. I've been interested in how the psychic and the social interact with one another, what unconscious cultural patterns we reproduce in sex, in politics, everywhere – and why we do that. The first step, now quite a long time ago, was a short paper on the Wolf Man case, which I presented at a seminar at the Jan van Eyck Academy in Maastricht in 2011. It was from this at that very chaotic presentation, focused on the topic of counting beasts not only in psychoanalysis but also in the Bible – in the Old Testament legend of Noah's Ark and the New Testament legend of the exorcism of demons – that the last chapter here, "The Number of Beasts," eventually grew.

Introduction 3

Later, in 2016–17, the outline of the chapter that appears first here and is called "The Theater of the Soul," began to develop. In this chapter, which is not about boys, but about girls, I am trying to describe – also through a personal example – the psychosexual knot of trauma, sexualized violence, fantasy, shame, and high moral standards within which our society is ultimately entangled.[1] It was difficult for me to write this chapter. It transgresses the boundaries – most of all my own – but I want it to serve as a sort of prolegomena to a philosophy of the girl that I would really love to be created someday by someone who would read and understand me properly. A disclaimer is needed here: in my work, any autobiographical material carries out certain conceptual tasks, but these are also moments of intrusion that break the theory rather than glue it together. Why shouldn't a theory be slightly broken? After all, this way it will be closer to what it theorizes.

In 2020–21, when the COVID pandemic caused terrible disruption worldwide, I turned to Freud again. Rereading his analysis of the obsessional neurosis in the Rat Man case, I drew attention to some parallels between social and psychic processes that occur in connection with external threats, such as the risk of infection, but also the threat of attack (structurally it is roughly the same thing; it is not by chance that the fight against the virus has been described as the war against an invisible enemy). Yes, the fear of contracting a deadly disease sounds rational, but if handwashing and other ways of creating protective barriers around ourselves turn into rituals that drive us into a frenzy, this might indicate that the real cause of our fear is not the virus, but something else – something that we are trying to forget, displace, or censor. This forgotten something, however, still has its proxy in our reality – say, a tiny animal that draws us into the darkness of the unconscious. We place the blame on this animal for all the sins, for spreading disease, bringing plague, and creating chaos: thus begins the hunt for rats (wolves, witches, and foreign agents).

4 Introduction

Some of my reflections on these symptoms were gathered together in an article on the problem of isolation not only in Freud, but also in Michel Foucault's analysis of the mechanisms of power. The article was published in 2021 in a Russian philosophy journal. However, two years after publication, in the course of political purges and censorship in academic and cultural spheres, the editors removed my name (together with the names of some other authors whose profiles did not fit the official state ideological trends) from the journal's website, thereby, ironically, demonstrating the mechanisms discussed in that article. Erasing my name was just one of the many sanitary procedures to which little contagious beasties like me were subjected in Russia.[2] After all, the deadly variety of passages between repression in the psychoanalytical, political, and merely police senses forced me to quit my position as a university professor and leave the country. In 2023, I ended up in Germany, where the title of this book – *Freud's Beasty Boys* – as well as the composition of the three Freudian cases emerged in my mind. It was then that I wrote the second chapter, "The Horse Is Being Beaten," about little Hans, a boy who was afraid of horses.

Those who are familiar with Freud's work will immediately guess that the title "A Horse Is Being Beaten" is a paraphrase of the title of his famous essay *A Child Is Being Beaten*, to which I do not refer directly, but there is certainly a connection between it and the cases analyzed here. Little Hans sees a horse being beaten, and his father calms him down, saying the horse does not feel pain. Before becoming afraid of horses, the child loves them, but he will grow up, become an adult man (a father), and learn to beat his own "horse" (someone defenseless) – or dominate in some other way – himself: this is the ritual. We might not recognize it as a ritual, but there it is: a surrogate victim mechanism, according to René Girard, or whatever else we might call the constitutive act of violence that sets the machine of masculinity in motion.

Introduction 5

I discuss this machine in the context not only of psychoanalysis, but also of anthropology and the history of religion, highlighting in each individual psycho-scenario a "totemic moment," that is, a moment of encounter and communication (traumatic or not) with whatever one's animal may be. It can be a symbolic or real encounter of some kind in which an exchange takes place, an encounter that triggers a disturbance or brings us into the state of affect. I call the totemic the moment when, sometimes without realizing it, we identify with an animal, reflect ourselves in it, or exchange perspectives with it – as if our own soul had appeared to us from outside in the guise of that animal. Wolves, rats, and horses are magical agents that connect us to the world of the dead, that is, to the tradition, the history of our people and culture, in which monotheism replaces (and represses) totemic practices, but some basic psychosocial matrix of turning love into violence does not cease to reproduce itself.

1

The Theater of the Soul

This book was written in the midst of a terrible war that tore my people apart. Some lost their jobs, families, friends, homes and homelands; others lost themselves. We were not prepared for this war; it came as a shock to us, and reduced all the diversity of life to the simplicity of death. Our population was divided into men and women, each group with its own task assigned to it by the rulers of the State: men – to be killed at war; and women – to give birth to new men. Other groups and individuals were forbidden, and those who shared different opinions or fell out of this binary code became illegal. The war – a triumphal march of the machine of masculinity – constitutes the background, but not the content, of this book. Also, behind this reflection is a nightmarish episode of my own biography, the memory of which does not allow me to understand, much less accept as destiny, the sexual difference in the form of the bad infinity of Eros and Thanatos imposed by the ideological apparatuses of the state.

As a teenager, I was sexually abused. At that time, I did not yet have any knowledge of sexuality and could not really understand what happened. The offence was

The Theater of the Soul

reported to the police, and, after a long trial during which I had to give endless evidence of that traumatic episode, the man was sentenced to jail for thirteen years. I always thought that this term was not long enough for him. Moreover, I believed that there is no term that could be enough, and even life imprisonment would have been insufficient. It's hard to forgive things like that; there is something unnatural about forgiveness. For my entire life I had to keep silent about that episode, because the general moral predisposition in the country where I lived implied that even if the man was in jail, it was me who was to blame. The possible stigma of being a bad girl could have ruined my socialization, studies, and future life.

This is certainly not something unique – many of my friends have been through something like this. In 2006 American activist Tarana Burke first used the phrase "Me Too," which became a slogan for solidarity and sisterhood of all girls with similar experiences, and, starting in 2017, was used as a hashtag for the social movement against sexualized violence, harassment, and abuse. Shortly before the actual beginning of the #MeToo campaign, in 2016, a Ukrainian journalist Anastasia Melnychenko wrote a post on Facebook under another hashtag – #IAmNotAfraidToSayIt – in which she reported on her own experience of abuse, and which gave rise to massive campaigns with the same agenda in Ukraine, Russia, and Belarus.[1] Thousands of people made public statements about having been sexually abused or harassed, and shared their memories of past traumatic events with varying degrees of severity – from a dirty look on the street or on public transport to actual or attempted rape – by strangers, spouses, parents, friends, relatives, friends of relatives, and relatives of friends.

The response to this wave of confessions has been ambivalent. Some pointed out that such discussion was long needed, that the level of aggression in society was extremely high, that the psychic trauma experienced by every second woman needed to be addressed, and that

8 The Theater of the Soul

bringing it into the public arena was positive, emancipatory, and contributed to democratization of communities in contrast to the conservative and patriarchal values imposed by the ideological apparatus of states like Russia, where violence against women is the norm. The confessions had an avalanche effect: even those who had never experienced such things found unpleasant or dubious episodes in their biography to add to the common dossier. The variety of negative sexual scenarios resulted in thousands of written stories whose details some readers delved into with indignation, others with excitement. There is no way to deny the latter: the fact is that the victim borrows the words used to speak of sexualized violence from everyday language, which is already infected by this very violence and more suited either for porn or for the evidence she has to give before the court, as if to justify herself. Have you read such evidence, made up of detailed descriptions of the sequence of movements of the bodies? Have you ever provided such evidence?

The survivor keeps silent not only because she is afraid of being shamed, but also because the pain she has experienced has turned her speech into an unarticulated animal scream or made her mute and now, in order to perform a speech act, she has to use the same alien tongue that once tried to worm its way into her mouth or whispered offensive words in her ear. The therapeutic effect of her public confession depends on whether this tongue will be re-appropriated by her, whether it will now become her ally, whether it will help her to react and, through speaking out, to recover from the trauma suffered in the past and then pushed to the periphery of her mental life.

Theoretical discussion of psychic traumas resulting from sexual abuse began at the end of the nineteenth century. Thus, the book *Studies on Hysteria*, written by Sigmund Freud and Josef Breuer in 1892, presents remarkable clinical records. It begins with a description of the case of Anna O. – a prominent feminist Bertha Pappenheim, who was a patient of Breuer. It was she who gave the name "talking

The Theater of the Soul 9

cure" or "chimney-sweeping" to a method of therapy that was at the time completely new and experimental.[2] Since antiquity, in accordance with etymology, the phenomenon of hysteria was often attributed to a "wandering uterus"[3] and other physiological factors. As Paul Verhaeghe recounts in his book on hysteria and psychoanalysis:

> Already in 2000 B.C., this theory was written down in a papyrus named *Kahun* after the place where it was discovered. It describes the uterus as an independent living organism. If not sufficiently irrigated, it becomes lighter and can start wandering around through the body, resulting in hysteria. Besides the number of very pragmatic tricks to get the uterus back to its proper place, the priest-doctors recommended marriage as a guarantee for the necessary "irrigation" that would keep the thing in its proper place.[4]

In Freud's time, hysteria was a popular diagnosis, and many doctors, including Freud himself (before the invention of psychoanalysis), tried to treat hysterics with electrotherapy and hypnosis. Psychoanalysis, by contrast, is born from the creative union of a patient, recognized in her subjectivity, and an analyst; from her active desire to speak out, to unburden her soul, and the readiness of an analyst to hear and understand. The origin of hysteria lies in the psychic life of a person: it is not the uterus that wanders in the body of a hysterical woman, but rather a memory of an experience so unbearable that it cannot be accepted in consciousness, a memory repressed, suppressed or displaced. According to Freud's initial hypothesis of the genesis of hysterical symptoms, it is this memory that indirectly causes arm and leg pain, cramps, tremors, syncope, and other symptoms: "Psychical trauma – or more precisely the memory of the trauma – acts like a foreign body which long after its entry must continue to be regarded as an agent that is still at work."[5] Psychic trauma is stuck in the body as a pathogenic agent for a long time: "*Hysterics suffer mainly from reminiscences.*"[6]

10   The Theater of the Soul

As noted by Verhaeghe: "Others had already observed that there was a traumatic etiology of hysteria. Nevertheless, Freud would be the first to listen to this trauma and to interpret it as having an effect on the psyche and hence on the soma."[7] After analyzing eighteen cases of hysteria, Freud concluded that the tormenting memories of the body referred to psychic traumas of a sexual character, with fear or agitation caused by irritation of the genitals in early childhood. Thus emerged the theory of seduction, according to which the origins of hysteria were traced back to nothing other than the sexual abuse of children, with the father figure looming over a vague image of an abuser in the memories of Freud's first patients.

One of the cases addressed by Freud in the *Studies on Hysteria* is called "typical." Its description takes only a few pages, as the analysis was unplanned and did not last more than a single session. In fact, it was not even a psychoanalytic session, but rather a random conversation with a young girl whom Freud met in the Austrian mountain resort of the Hohe Tauern, where he had come on holiday: "to forget medicine and more particularly the neuroses."[8] Finding out that he was a doctor, this young girl, Katharina (Aurelia Kronich) approached Freud in person and complained of the panic attacks she had been suffering from for the past two years. During the conversation, as if by chance, Freud suggested: "At that time, two years ago, you must have seen or heard something that very much embarrassed you, and that you'd much rather not have seen."[9] Katharina confirmed that about two years previously, when she was sixteen, she had discovered her uncle with her cousin, and noted that her first panic attack had occurred at the same time. After she had told her aunt about the incident, a family drama and a divorce ensued. In Freud's understanding, what the girl actually meant by the ancle and the aunt was her father and mother. The "aunt" and Katharina moved away together, leaving the "uncle" alone with the cousin who, by that point, was already pregnant. This memory suddenly awakened in Katharina's

The Theater of the Soul · 11

mind another experience from an even earlier period of her life. At the age of fourteen, she happened to have been sexually harassed by that very same "uncle": one night he took the opportunity to crawl into the girl's bed. She was frightened "feeling his body in the bed"[10] without being aware of what was going on.

This description introduces a specific temporality to the genesis of hysteria. It is the belatedness of the symptom in relation to the first sexual trauma, which, according to Freud, makes Katharina's case typical. She turns hysterical not right after being abused as a child, but only after she learns about sexuality: "In every analysis of a case of hysteria based on sexual traumas we find that impressions from the pre-sexual period which produced no effect on the child and attain traumatic power at a later date as memories, when the girl or married woman has acquired an understanding of sexual life."[11] A single trauma is not enough to trigger a hysterical symptom: a repetition is also necessary. The abuse or seduction happens more than once: first the child, who has no knowledge of sexuality and does not yet understand what is going on, is subjected to it – and then the adolescent, in whom the awakening of sexuality resurrects the memory of the traumatic episode, makes it truly pathogenic. Thus, the primary, original trauma occurs through the mediation of a second one, which Freud calls "auxiliary," but which, as he states, has its own content and "deserves equally to be called 'traumatic.'"[12]

The idea that the second trauma may precede the first one reveals two inseparable characteristics constitutive for the psychoanalytic interpretation not only of the mechanism of the trauma, but also of the structure of psychic time itself: retroactivity and repetition. The time of traumatic eventuality, or psychic time, moves backwards as if in a circle. Retroactivity and repetition are a time bomb embedded in the foundation of reality. If the repeated (trauma I) is born through the act of repetition itself (trauma II), then the reality is set up like a stage play. As noted by Alenka Zupančič: "In theater, we start with 'repetitions,'

12 The Theater of the Soul

for rehearsals are called *repetitions*, and we end up with *la première*, with the first (performance or the first night). Repetitions do not repeat some first occurrence but, rather, lead up to it."[13] It is no accident that meaningful episodes of a person's psychic life are described by Freud as scenes. We are dealing with a theater of the soul, with its plots, actors, characters, scenes and backstages. The dirty scene of the uncle seducing the cousin can thus be interpreted as a rehearsal of the seduction of Katharina herself, which would have taken place two years earlier.

In 1896, in the paper entitled "The etiology of hysteria," presented at the Vienna Society for Psychiatry and Neurology, Freud proposed the arguments for his theory of seduction. The talk was received coldly by the audience. Famous psychiatrist Richard von Krafft-Ebing, who was presiding the meeting, called it "a scientific fairy tale."[14] At first, Freud regarded this cold reception as a resistance of the academic community to accepting an uncomfortable truth. However, already in 1897, the analyst himself lost confidence in his own theory. Something did not work with the hypothesis, so contradictory to common sense: how could it be possible that so many good fathers were actually abusers? This just could not be true! In the end, Freud had to admit that "such widespread perversion against children is scarcely probable."[15]

The question remained, however, as to what to make of the patients' confessions? Freud's next suggestion was that childhood screen memories, with or without sexual content, could have been constructed. What was at stake was not reality, but unconscious fantasies. Much later, in 1933, in his paper untitled "Femininity," he recounts: "In the period in which the main interest was directed to discovering infantile sexual traumas, almost all my women patients told me that they had been seduced by their father. I was driven to recognize in the end that these reports were untrue and so came to understand that hysterical symptoms are derived from phantasies and not from real occurrences."[16]

The Theater of the Soul 13

Let me give you one example of a constructed memory from my personal life. I don't think it contains any sexual connotation, but not that Freud would have agreed with me on this point. When I was a little girl, my mother took me on a trip to Bishkek (then called Frunze). There we visited the zoo, and that was the first time I saw elephants. I can't say exactly how many elephants there were, because I didn't know how to count yet, but I guess about five. The elephants were huge, like five-story buildings, and very dark, almost black. My mom, other visitors and I would throw them gingerbread and they would catch it with their trunks. All of my life I lived with this memory, but when, more than forty years later, I came to Bishkek again, I discovered that neither the zoo nor the elephants had ever been in this city. That came as a shock, as I had never questioned the reality of this memory. My mother confirmed that we had neither visited the zoo nor seen elephants, though we had seen camels in the steppe, and perhaps in my memory the camels had somehow turned into elephants.

Back to Freud: the idea that infantile memories might be products of imagination does not, however, lessen their importance. On the contrary, for the analysis, the fantasmatic reality turns out to be even more significant than the real fact: "It remains a fact that the patient has created these phantasies for himself, and this fact is of scarcely less importance for his neurosis than if he had really experienced what the phantasies contain. The phantasies possess *psychical* as contrasted with *material* reality, and we gradually learn to understand that *in the world of the neuroses it is psychical reality which is the decisive kind.*"[17] The theater of the soul is made up of scenes constituting a psychic reality, which encompasses subjects and enables the variety of their neurotic perspectives.

The seduction or abuse of a girl by her father is not the only way in which the link between material reality and psychic reality is called into question in Freud's writings. Among the motifs discussed in connection to infantile

14 The Theater of the Soul

fantasies, he lists "observation of parental intercourse, seduction by an adult and threat of being castrated."[18] In his later lectures on psychoanalysis, Freud draws attention to the fact that these fantasies, regardless of the extent to which they may correspond to reality, appear with a kind of necessity:

> The only impression we gain is that these events of childhood are somehow demanded as a necessity, that they are among the essential elements of a neurosis. If they have occurred in reality, so much to the good; but if they have been withheld by reality, they are put together from hints and supplemented by phantasy. The outcome is the same, and up to the present we have not succeeded in pointing to any difference in the consequences, whether phantasy or reality has had the greater share in these events of childhood.[19]

These reflections make me think about one recent telling example. In 2019, a thirteen-year-old schoolgirl from the town of Zelenograd (near Moscow) reported to the police that she had been raped by five adult men on her way to school. The girl claimed that the rape took place in a car parked next to a children's health center. However, after reviewing the surveillance camera footage, police officers discovered that she had calmly walked to school without getting into any cars and then returned home without incident as well. Medical examination revealed no traces of violence.[20] Freud's theory of psychic reality provides a key to understanding this case, which otherwise sounds strange, to say the least. The act of rape takes place not in the material reality documented by the security cameras but in a fantasmatic reality of which the observer is not even aware. Even if the girl makes it safely to school and back, the effect is the same as if she was really raped by those five imaginary men. The fantasy becomes a part of subjective experience and is not only incorporated into it, but can also structure it. We live in a society where, even if no one abused us, we were still abused. Even if this never

The Theater of the Soul 15

happened, it still happened. This is what I call the theater of the soul: with a kind of necessity, psychic reality adjusts to some obsessive fantasmatic scenarios which we complete ourselves with our own scenes. Why are we doing that?

According to Freud, such fantasies or screen memories, which are mostly indirect, like allusions, refer to unconscious desires that adult people would never recognize as their own, and that would never get through the inner censorship whose function is to adapt our drives to the rules and requirements of human society. Obsessional neurosis, hysteria, phobia, and other distortions of psychic life have their origins in childhood, in a nuclear family, which Freud understands as an oedipal triangle determining girls and boys to follow different paths of desire. In 1905, Freud publishes his *Three Essays on the Theory of Sexuality*, and in the second of these three essays introduces the concept of infantile sexuality, which replaces the earlier trauma theory.[21] In this new perspective, we are separated from the period of our childhood by infantile amnesia, which prevents us from understanding children as subjects already enjoying their polymorphous sexuality originating in bodily contact with their parents.

However, even with this new perspective, trauma theory never vanishes completely. The idea that parents touch children when taking care of them and that children might actually enjoy this to such an extent that they develop sexual fantasies which would later cause neural or psychic disorders, cannot be sufficient to explain the content of these fantasies. Still, according to Freud, something should have really happened – just maybe *not in our life*. Hence comes his engagement with myths, Greek tragedy, and speculations on prehistory.

An important place in this series is taken by the story of parricide presented in *Totem and Taboo*: a group of brothers unites, kills – and devours! – a brutal alpha male, the father of the primal horde, and this collective act of transgression marks the beginning of an entire Western culture

16 The Theater of the Soul

based on the prohibition of incest and cannibalism.[22] This myth, invented by Freud himself, sounds more realistic if we think of a ritual animal sacrifice in an ancient religions: a totem animal – say, a bear – is the god, the soul, and the great forefather of the tribe, and at the same time the one who must be killed in the festive scene of a tribal communion. One might suggest that the father of the primal horde also became a sacrificial animal. However, according to Freud, parricide precedes sacrificial religion: the totem animal comes as a surrogate for the father.

What all Freudian myths have in common is that they have a sexual content, challenge the concept of the family and gender structure, and refer to the past (be it individual childhood story or collective prehistory of humankind). The reality of these events is ultimately doubtful, yet their variations are endlessly repeated in our psychic complexes. As explained by Octave Mannoni: "the need to find real experiences behind the fantasies induced Freud in this account to go so far as to formulate a hypothesis that he was never to abandon, namely, one of species memory, of a phylogenetic heritage."[23] This is how Freud formulates it in his lecture on the formation of symptoms:

> Whence comes the need for these phantasies and the material for them? There can be no doubt that their sources lie in the instincts; but it has still to be explained why the same phantasies with the same content are created on every occasion. I am prepared with an answer, which I know will seem daring to you. I believe these *primal phantasies*, as I should like to call them, and no doubt a few others as well, are a phylogenetic endowment. In them the individual reaches beyond his own experience into primeval experience at points where his own experience has been too rudimentary. It seems to me quite possible that all the things that are told to us today in analysis as phantasy – the seduction of children, the inflaming of sexual excitement by observing parental intercourse, the threat of castration (or rather castration itself) – were once real occurrences in the primeval times of the human family, and that children in

The Theater of the Soul 17

their phantasies are simply filling in the gaps in individual truth with prehistoric truth.[24]

Thus, the origin of trauma, just like the origin of fantasy, according to Freud, is phylogenetic. The theater of the soul, on the stage of which we rehearse the scenes of incest or parricide, transcends the boundaries of individual life and traces back to ancient communities, to the generic and species being of human animals. This in itself is an extremely interesting line of thought, where psychoanalysis borders cultural and philosophical anthropology and offers its own versions of anthropogenesis. Freud is concerned about the prehistoric past because he wants to understand the origins of sexuality, family structure, and the distribution of gender roles. But this is only a theoretical side of his engagement with myths. What is more important for him as a doctor is a practical, clinical side. One should not forget that Freud's analysis is oriented towards psychological treatment, for which a story must be provided, and this is a story of desire; a sexual narrative. It is in this context that Freud's vector of interpreting hysteria moves from real abuse or seduction to the patient's own unconscious fantasies. It starts by seeking for a cause of the patient's physical suffering in her own libido, repressed, disguised as memory, and finally converted into a distressing symptom.

I am trying to imagine that academic gathering in Vienna: psychiatrists, neurologists, eminent professors, men of science in dark suits; Freud reading his paper on the etiology of hysteria and trying to be as convincing as possible, although he himself knows that the hypothesis of seduction that he presents sounds unbelievable. The message is too radical for this public. He would have opened a #metoo Pandora's box way back in 1897, but his ideas did not find any support. In this regard, Freud's disavowal of the seduction theory and shifting the vector of his investigation towards infantile sexuality – that is, as it were, from the materiality of abuse to the fantasmatic theater of the patient's own desire – looks like an act of surrendering to

18   The Theater of the Soul

the status quo.[25] The reputation of good fathers has not been damaged, the only people to blame were girls themselves, for fantasizing something that made them suffer. Much later, one of Freud's disciples, Sandor Ferenczi, argued that Freud's early seduction hypothesis was correct. Not only did Ferenczi believe women's accounts of having been sexually abused as children, but also his male patients confirmed that they were really abusing children. As he observed in his paper "Confusion of tongues between adults and the child": "Even children of very respectable, sincerely puritanical families, fall victim to real violence or rape much more often than one had dared to suppose."[26]

At this point, one could immediately call to "cancel" Freud, forget his writings and his name. But I think this would be imprudent. The strength of Freud's theory is that it is really efficient in uncovering the patriarchal structure which he did not, however, seriously problematize as such. Freud analyzes fantasies of being seduced or abused; he suggests factors which might cause these fantasies, claims that they are no less important than real facts, and explains why they are important: because they have real effects on the body, but also because they connect individual experiences with the life of the species and the very origins of humanity. In my perspective, the problem is not that Freud succumbs to the common sense of his time and suggests that his hysterical patients pretend their fantasies are real facts, but that his analysis is limited by sexuality and does not try to go beyond this limit. The persistence of fantasies can be a sign of something else. What if sexuality is not a solution, not an answer to the question posed by hysteria or other psychic disorders, but rather a distortion, something that prevents us from learning the truth? What do screen memories screen? Scenes and episodes the content of which is disclosed as sexual, but something is still lurking behind the scene.

I wish I could say that, just like those hysterical fantasies, my memory of a sexual abuse was fake too. Moreover, sometimes I still doubt whether or not it actually hap-

The Theater of the Soul 19

pened. However, there is some evidence that can make other people admit the fact of this accident (the simplest criterion of distinction between reality and fantasy: something is taking place both for myself and for others). When the lawyer suggested to the court that it was my own desire to be abused – as if he had read Freud and taken him too literally, thus entirely missing the point – he implicitly committed himself to the surplus enjoyment of the abuser insofar as the latter enjoyed attributing unconscious sexual desire to a child and sought to satisfy it. While my infantile sexuality was apparently projected into me by these adult men, in actual fact, I did have a desire, but not the one they thought I had. In my memories (the worst of them is that there was a baby crib in that bedroom: that's why I don't have children; the sight of baby cribs makes me sick), I return to one particular episode again and again.

The compulsion to repeat, which he observed in people suffering from post-traumatic disorder who constantly returned in their nightmares to the negative experiences that they survived in the past, Freud connected to the death drive – an unconscious striving toward homeostasis or a move to a previous state of existence.[27] Rebecca Comay interprets it as "the desire to return to a time before the beginning – to go back not for the sake of regressing but in order to take it over again, to do it otherwise."[28] So I return to my own traumatic experience not in order to reproduce it, but in order to undo it, to make it un-happen. The moment in time that I am trying to retrace is not the scene of rape itself, but the one that precedes it: the man let me in and locked the door; then we went to the kitchen; there was a knife there: I could have taken that knife, attacked him first and defended myself. This is an alternative scenario, which is rehearsed in my fantasy for the psychic theater. But I am only 13 years old and he is 26: our chances are unequal. Perhaps, I had an intention to attack, but quickly calculated the options and surrendered, delegating to the state penitentiary system my desire for revenge, or, in other words, appealing to the apparatuses

20 The Theater of the Soul

of police violence against an individual act of sexualized violence.

Freud is aware of the Thanatos which sexuality tries to soften by screening our fantasies as memories or memories as fantasies. Beyond that, I tend to read his research into the infantile psyche as an invitation to break this screen. Along these lines, I propose to re-examine three famous cases from Freud's psychoanalytic practice in the context of the relationship between sex and violence. What these three stories have in common is that they all involve animals: little Hans with his horse phobia (1909), the Rat Man (1909) and the Wolf Man (1918) are beasty boys. In their cases, an analysis of anxiety or fear, associated with a particular kind of animal, brings Freud to the Oedipus family triangle and to the ambiguous emotional attitudes of boys toward their fathers. In all cases, animals serve as a prop to locate oedipal projections and fantasies. The psychic theater suggests different scenarios for boys and girls, but I am focusing on the roles performed by animals in these screenplays, and on possible trajectories of animality beyond the sexual content revealed by Freud.

2

A Horse Is Being Beaten

In 1909, Freud published his *Analysis of a Phobia in a Five-Year-Old Boy*, a study known as the case of Little Hans. Hans (Herbert Graf) was not among Freud's patients. Instead, his father, the Austrian critic and museologist Max Graf, a friend of Freud and enthusiastic admirer of his method, played the role of the boy's psychoanalyst. Luckily, Hans's parents were very liberal in their educational strategies, and treated the boy with a lot of respect and confidence. The father followed every detail of his son's psychic development with great attention, especially when it came to sexuality. Thus, he shares with Freud his observations about Hans's increased interest in the genitals: a three-year-old boy keeps interrogating his parents about the thing he calls "Wiwimacher,"[1] speculates on big and small Wiwimachers in different kinds of animals including humans, and creates a hypothesis that all living beings have Wiwimachers.

From the very beginning, this moment introduces a misunderstanding in the ongoing dialog between the father and the son. Indeed, Hans is right: most living beings have Wiwimachers, by which he understands, as the word says, the organs of urinating. This hypothesis is also confirmed by his mother, whom he asks whether she, too, has a Wiwimacher. According to Hans, big animals, like horses or giraffes, have big Wiwimachers, and small animals have small ones. He does not yet divide people into two sexes, and is equally social and tender with boys and girls. He expects that his mother would have a bigger Wiwimacher, like a horse, but this suggestion cannot be confirmed, as he never sees her naked. When he observes his newborn sister being given a bath, he remarks that her Wiwimacher is tiny, but that it will grow bigger. Later, he will laugh at his sister's organ, but also call it "lovely."[2]

Hans's father, however, adopts a different opinion. In his perspective, only males have Wiwimachers, and the bigger the male, the bigger the Wiwimacher (along these lines, he does not miss a chance to emphasize that his own organ is bigger[3]). It is not that the father does not know that females also urinate and indeed have organs to do so (as his son observes in accompanying his mother when she goes to the toilet). Of course, he knows, but somehow neglects it, since all his line of argumentation derives from a misconception: he thinks that Wiwimacher is a penis, and tries to convince Hans of this.[4] It should also be noted that the father attributes to the penis a sexual and reproductive function, of which Hans is not yet aware, rather than the urinary one.

It is no surprise that Freud, who consults Hans's father and gives him some analytic advice, shares his conceptual blindness and supports the penis theory, the inconsistency of which might create a cognitive dissonance in a child whose mental openness and fluidity is not yet restricted by gender socialization. Freud himself seems to have this aberration: he relies too heavily on the symbolism of the absence of penis in women, and believes that for children this must also be a decisive factor in their self-identification. Anyway, the father and the son engage into an ongoing dialog around Wiwimacher and related subjects, and their interest turns out to be not exclusively theoretical, but also

A Horse Is Being Beaten 23

practical, if by practice is meant the boy's early attempts at masturbation from which both Hans's parents try to discourage him.

This is what is presented as the background to when, at a certain point in time, the boy becomes afraid of horses. The fear comes in many guises, but the figure of the horse is always in play. He is afraid that a horse will enter the room, that a horse will bite him, and, finally, that a horse will fall and die. As a result, the boy doesn't want to go outside where there are horses. He would stay at home, close to his mother who would take him into her bed. Of course, Max connects Hans's fear to his having observed a horse's Wiwimacher, and, with Freud's Oedipus schematism in mind, claims that, for Hans, a horse replaces him, the father. One of his interpretations suggests that the boy is scared that the father-horse with a big Wiwimacher will enter the room, where he (Hans) does something secret with his mother, which he does not yet know the name for. Freud provides more such scenarios in which one can read sexual subtexts. They include Han's fear that the horse can bite as fear of castration. Another fantasy, that a horse will fall and die, is interpreted as camouflaging the child's unconscious oedipal wish that his father would fall down and die. He also imagines his mother as a horse who falls because she is too heavy, bearing a heavy carriage, that is, she is pregnant. A falling horse can equally be a baby, his sister, who falls like feces from his mother's body. There is also a maid, who "lets him ride on her back while she cleans the floor," and whom he calls "my horse."[5] Finally, there is his friend Fritzl whom he sees fall while they play at being horses.[6]

In short, we are presented with a kaleidoscope of associations, in which everybody in Hans's surroundings, including Hans himself, features as a horse. It is as if his fear opened another dimension of reality – a theater of the soul, in which all people were played by horses. It is notable that the persistent attempts by Hans's father, and by Freud, to organize this material around one single narrative and

24 A Horse Is Being Beaten

to find out which of Hans's family is "really" a horse repeatedly collapse, as the new characters with horse faces enter the stage. We are in a horse theater. One should not forget that the story takes place in the early 1900s, before the advent of the era of automobiles and other modern means of motorized transport. At that time, horses were an indispensable part of all urban or rural communities; they were literally everywhere, carrying people and goods of all kinds. Where there were people, there were horses as well. Nowadays, when horses are much less present, fear of them could easily remained unnoticed, but little Hans sees many horses every day. This is why his phobia is so troublesome: it really gets in the way of normal life.

Freud suggests the term "anxiety-hysteria" to define phobias such as the one suffered by little Hans. In his perspective, this term

> finds its justification in the similarity between the psychological structure of these phobias and that of hysteria – a similarity which is complete except upon a single point. That point, however, is a decisive one and well adapted for purposes of differentiation. For in anxiety-hysteria the libido which has been liberated from the pathogenic material by repression is not *converted* (that is, diverted from the mental[7] sphere into a somatic innervation), but is set free in the shape of *anxiety*.[8]

This differentiation is based on his theory of infantile sexuality, according to which hysteria is caused by the libido (and not by externally caused trauma, as he originally assumed). Whereas in hysteria libido converts into a wandering symptom in the body, in anxiety-hysteria it becomes fear. Freud notes that such psychoneurotic disorders are the most common and appear in the earliest periods of life: "they are *par excellence* the neuroses of childhood."[9]

According to Freud, at first, anxiety into which the libido is released appears like an empty shell that can be filled with any content: an object of fear is secondary to the fear itself. Thus, Freud explains Hans's anxiety in terms

A Horse Is Being Beaten

of his attraction to his mother succumbing to repression and turning into anxiety. At first it was, "like every infantile anxiety, without an object to begin with: it was still anxiety and not yet fear."[10] The boy did not even know what exactly he feared, until his anxiety assigned it to a pretty much random object. It is perhaps the omnipresence of horses that can explain why little Hans chooses this particular animal to be afraid of. However, the question remains, what exactly could have triggered his phobia? His father begins with the hypothesis that Hans's fear that a horse might bite him could have been related to his having seen a horse with a large penis.[11] But the boy also has real grounds to be afraid of a horse biting him: he had overheard someone saying that if one puts one's finger on a horse, it will bite (an outcome that Hans's father interprets in terms of the fear of castration). Through further conversation, more details emerge and modify the initial scenario.

One detail is especially important. The family's home is located near "the warehouse of the Office for the Taxation of Food-Stuffs, with a loading dock at which carts are driving up all day long to fetch away boxes, packing-cases, etc.," says Hans's father. "This courtyard is cut off from the street by railings; and the entrance gates to the courtyard are opposite our house,"[12] he adds.

After giving this description, the father brings up an important episode from the case history: "I have noticed for some days that Hans is specially frightened when carts drive into or out of the yard, a process which involves their taking a corner. I asked at the time why he was so much afraid, and he replied: '*I'm afraid the horses will fall down when the cart turns.*'"[13] In a later conversation Hans provides a further explanation of the origin of his phobia, which he calls "nonsense" – and this is not a fantasy, but a real accident: the boy recalls that once, when he was out for a walk with his mother, he saw a horse that was drawing a big bus fall over and flail its legs, at which he was scared and thought the horse was dead. This led to the following conversation, recounted by the father[14]:

26 A Horse Is Being Beaten

Hans: And I'm most afraid of furniture-vans, too.

I: Why?

Hans: I think when furniture-horses are dragging a heavy van they'll fall down.

I: So, you're not afraid with a small cart?

Hans: No. I'm not afraid with a small cart or with a post-office van. I'm most afraid too when a bus comes along.

I: Why? Because it's so big?

Hans: No. Because once a horse in a bus fell down.

I: When?

Hans: Once when I went out with Mummy in spite of my "nonsense," when I bought the waistcoat. (This was subsequently confirmed by his mother.)

I: What did you think when the horse fell down?

Hans: Now it'll always be like this. All horses in buses will fall down.

I: In all buses?

Hans: Yes. And in furniture-vans too. Not often in furniture-vans.

I: You had your nonsense already at that time?

Hans: No. I only got it then. When the horse in the bus fell down, it gave me such a fright, really! That was when I got the nonsense.[15]

Apparently, Hans's idea that a horse would fall down differs from his previous fear of being bitten by a horse. However, in the same dialog Hans finds a way to reconcile these two aspects of his phobia, each of which is thus grounded in reality: one time he was told that a horse would bite his fingers, another time he witnessed a horse fall. This prompts his father to tell Hans: "But the nonsense was that you thought a horse would bite you. And now you say you were afraid a horse would fall down." To which Hans adds: "Fall down and bite."[16]

Freud notes that the episode with the fallen horse "immediately preceded the outbreak of the illness and may no doubt be regarded as the precipitating cause of its outbreak."[17] At that point, one would assume that the source of Hans's "anxiety-hysteria" might not be the libido but psychic trauma, as Freud's earlier hypothesis would seem to suggest. However, he regards this episode as "insignificant in itself"[18] and as carrying "no traumatic force."[19] According to Freud, what is needed for the formation of a symptom is a set of associations and fantasies, particularly involving the boy's family members. Fallen horse is not the only real occurrence that he witnessed: some time earlier he saw his beloved friend Fritzl falling and bleeding when they were playing at being horses. This event, according to Freud, has "more claim to be regarded as traumatic," and creates "an easy path of association from Fritzl to his father."[20] Hans is lured down this path by Max, who continues the conversation by pushing him to acknowledge that when the boy saw a horse fall down "he must have thought of him, his father, and have wished that he might fall down in the same way and be dead."[21] Thus the "insignificant" story of a fallen horse on the street is wrapped up in the plot of the Greek myth, and little Hans becomes little Oedipus destined to kill his father. The boy accepts his proposed role in this scenario and lets his father proceed with his narrative.[22]

Further along, new details emerge. One day Hans says, pointing at the loading dock of the courtyard across the street: "When a cart stands there, I'm afraid I shall tease the horses and they'll fall down and make a row with their feet."[23] What does the boy mean by teasing the horses? Shouting "Gee-up," but also whipping them. A horse falls after being whipped, or: a horse is being whipped until it falls. The father keeps interrogating:

I: But you like teasing them?
Hans: Oh yes, very much.
I: Would you like to whip them?
Hans: Yes.
I: Would you like to beat the horses as Mummy beats Hanna? You like that too, you know.
Hans: It doesn't do the horses any harm when they're beaten.[24]

28 A Horse Is Being Beaten

The last statement is provided with father's brief explication in parenthesis: "I said this to him once to mitigate his fear of seeing horses whipped."[25] I would like to focus on this moment, which seems to be comprehended neither by Freud, nor by the father: Hans did not only see a horse fallen, but also a horse being beaten. Is this scene of cruelty still less traumatic and less significant than the oedipal fantasies that immediately replace it in the father's narrative? Why is the boy at first scared to see a horse being beaten? Because he rightly perceives that the horse is hurt – until he is persuaded by his father that it is not. But the father lies: the horse is actually hurt. What if it is a child's immediate compassionate impulse, a sensitivity to other's pain, and not an unconscious desire to kill the father and sleep with the mother, that is thus being repressed and becomes phobia?

We have to understand that at that time horses were not only omnipresent, but also widely exploited and abused, and violence against them was commonplace. Like many animals, they were treated not as complex sentient creatures, but as mere commodities and means of transport. In the poem "Kindness to horses," written in 1918, Soviet poet Vladimir Mayakovsky describes the scene of a horse falling down on a street in Moscow. A crowd of people immediately gathers and starts laughing at the animal, but the poet does not share this collective attitude. Instead, he approaches and sees tears in the horse's eyes:

I came up and saw
tears, – huge and passionate,
rolling down the face,
vanishing in its coat . . .
and some kind of a universal,
animal anguish
spilled out of me
and splashing, it flowed.
"Horse, there's no need for this!
Horse, listen, –
look at them all, – who has it worse?

> Child,
> we are all, to some extent, horses, –
> everyone here is a bit of a horse."[26]

A child as little as Hans might share with the poet kindness and sensitivity that many adults have lost. He might not really distinguish between humans and other animals; he plays at horses and claims: "I'm a young horse."[27] It is a sense of the deep affinity of all living beings, which is given to him intimately and directly, that is reflected in his Wiwimacher saga. Doesn't his claim that all living beings have Wiwimachers echo Aristotelian naturalism, according to which all living beings have souls? Doesn't Wiwimacher as a common attribute of all animals stand for the soul in little Hans's materialist philosophy? A horse has a big one, he himself a small one, his sister has a lovely one and so on. That is why a child is so full of empathy: in his universe, a horse is not an inanimate thing; it might be a friend, a relative, a fellow being.

The father might not even take this compassion seriously. He does not seem to care about horses and is only receptive to an adult, sexual content strictly centered around phallic signifiers. Trying to protect Hans's feelings and pacify his fear, he at the same time teaches the boy to perceive the scene of animal abuse as something ordinary and normal. Illness, fear might arise as a response to the terror of such normality, to which one has to adapt in order to become a member of human society. Hans's father's claim that horses do not get hurt sounds like a lesson in Cartesianism, for it was Descartes who famously claimed that animals have no souls, and their bodies are mere machines that do not feel pain. Think about Nietzsche's madness as an ultimate experience of rejection of such a lesson. Thus, Milan Kundera refers to the tragic episode in Turin, when Nietzsche witnessed the scene of a merchant beating his horse:

> Seeing a horse and a coachman beating it with a whip, Nietzsche went up to the horse and, before the coachman's

very eyes, put his arms around the horse's neck and burst into tears. That took place in 1889, when Nietzsche, too, had removed himself from the world of people. In other words, it was at the time when his mental illness had just erupted. But for that very reason I feel his gesture has broad implications: Nietzsche was trying to apologize to the horse for Descartes. His lunacy (that is, his final break with mankind) began at the very moment he burst into tears over the horse.[28]

The scene ends with Nietzsche losing consciousness. Then follows an exacerbation of mental illness, after which he never recovers. Crying for the horse, he abandons language and withdraws from the world of humans. All attempts to make him return to normality fail, since he had unlearned playing by the rules of the game. Unlike Nietzsche, little Hans wants to recover from his "nonsense," and is very good at learning Cartesian lessons, even better than his father would expect. After repeating his father's mantra that whipping does not do harm to horses, the boy suddenly claims: "Once I had the whip, and whipped the horse, and it fell down and made a row with its feet."[29] This sounds improbable, and soon in the conversation with his father it is revealed that the boy made the whole thing up:

Hans: *What I've told you isn't the least true.*
I: How much of it is true?
Hans: None of it is true; I only told it you for fun.
I: You never took a horse out of the stables?
Hans: Oh no.
I: But you wanted to.
Hans: Oh yes, wanted to. I've thought it to myself.[30]

The scene of Hans himself whipping a horse is already a product of his fantasy, which then immediately takes a libidinal direction with his saying of his mother: "I should just like to beat her."[31] Thus, with the active assistance of his father, the child makes the journey from empathy to cruelty, from compassion to sadistic fantasies, from being

A Horse Is Being Beaten

a horse to beating a horse. Between these two states, he bites like a horse, which, in his father's interpretation, corresponds to identification with the father: "For some time Hans has been playing horses in the room; he trots about, falls down, kicks about with his feet, and neighs. Once he tied a small bag on like a nose-bag. He has repeatedly run up to me and bitten me," Max reported. "Thus *he* was the horse, and bit his father, and in this way was identifying himself with his father,"[32] interpreted Freud. In the father's perspective, such identification relates to the threat of castration, which the boy received from his parents when he attempted to masturbate, and which was then associated with another threat – that a horse will bite his fingers: this altogether becomes a fearful fantasy that the horse-father will enter the room and bite. But what if, by falling down, kicking with his feet and biting his father, Hans the horse not only identifies with him, but also, and in the first place, rebels against him – rebels like a horse?

The father invites the son to make a passage from a queer multispecies childish world to the adult normality of binary distinctions – humans and animals, men and women – ruled by the paternal law which implies a hierarchical family structure and authorizes violence against horses, women, or children. The passage from one realm to another is marked by sexuality, which smooths the terror of seeing an animal beaten and/or fallen, and hides it behind the veil of eroticism and phallic symbolism. The child is trying to say that the horse falls, but the father immediately replaces his pity which is bursting out with an all-too-human erotic story of desire and jealousy within a family triangle. "Hans was playing with a little toy horse. At that moment the horse fell down, and Hans shouted out: 'The horse has fallen down! Look what a row it's making!',", his father reported before adding the following conversation between himself and Hans:

I: You're a little vexed with Daddy because Mummy's fond of him.

32   A Horse Is Being Beaten

Hans: No.
I: Then why do you always cry whenever Mummy gives me
  a kiss? It's because you're jealous.
Hans: Jealous, yes.
I: You'd like to be Daddy yourself.
Hans: Oh yes.[33]

Again, throughout these conversations, the father literally imposes the role of Oedipus on his son and attempts to trace his own presence in all Hans's fantasies. He keeps suggesting to the child that he (Hans) wants to take his (father's) place and become a father himself, even when the boy expresses his absolutely fascinating desire to become a mother, give birth to multiple children and take care of them.[34] One should not forget that this is a progressive intelligent family, where, in contrast to many other bourgeois families, it is supposed that infantile sexuality is not repressed, but openly discussed in a very emancipated and democratic manner. And it is true, indeed it is amazing, how open and supportive the parents are, for whom nothing seems forbidden and who open the door for a free flight of thought which really helps Hans to overcome his childish fear.

My argument, however, is that something is getting lost on this road to normality. Namely, before sex – or beyond sex – there is a kind of *horseness* which does not supplement the Oedipal family narrative, but rather competes with it. And it is this horseness that becomes exposed to violence: not a physical violence which is applied to real horses on a regular basis, but – to borrow Slavoj Žižek's definition – a symbolic violence, that is, the violence of language itself,[35] which subordinates subjects to already existing ideological structures (and, in our case, produces men and women out of the queer animality of children). Symbolic violence is invisible, but the physical violence that we can see – for instance, against animals that supposedly do not feel pain – can be regarded as the effect of it, because symbolic structures frame the limits of possible

A Horse Is Being Beaten 33

and legitimate social practices. Thus, through the sexual narrative, the father indoctrinates his son into the dominant ideology and teaches him to live in the world where horses are being beaten.

Meanwhile, the relationship between horses and education is not so simple if one recalls another case that belongs to the same historical period. If Hans and his father were to travel from Austria to Germany, they could have met there an extraordinary horse named Clever Hans. In 1904, following the issue in *The New York Times* under the headline "Berlin's Wonderful Horse,"[36] it became known to the world as the animal who was able to perform intellectual tasks of various degrees of complexity, such as counting, and gave correct answers to different questions with gestures such as stepping his hoofs a specified number of times. His owner, Wilhelm von Osten, a math teacher and amateur horse trainer, was travelling throughout the country and exhibiting Hans's performances without charging the public. He wanted to show that horses are smart creatures and can exhibit their intelligence if they are trained "from a scientific standpoint."[37]

Note that at that time, especially after the publication of Darwin's *On the Origin of Species* in 1859, an intellectual trend has emerged to reconsider psychic life and cognitive capacities in animals, and cases like this have drawn much attention. In 1904, a special commission was appointed by the German Board of Education: a group of experts that consisted of a veterinarian, a circus manager, a cavalry officer, the director of the zoological garden, and some schoolteachers had come together to decide whether Clever Hans was really intelligent, or just learned some tricks. As the newspaper reports: "The commission has issued a statement declaring that it is of the opinion that there is no trickery whatever in the performances of the horse, and that the methods employed by the owner, Herr von Osten, in teaching Hans differ essentially from those used by trainers, and correspond with those used in teaching children in elementary schools."[38] Thus, admittedly,

34 A Horse Is Being Beaten

Clever Hans was not trained as a horse, but educated as a human being.

However, in 1907, another investigation was undertaken by German biologist and psychologist Oskar Pfungst, who, after conducting a few experiments with Hans, demonstrated that the horse did not really answer the questions, but rather reacted to some involuntary clues, produced by the body language of the trainer. In this perspective, Hans was clever not in that he solved arithmetic problems, but in that he could decipher unconscious signals and signs sent by his owner or someone else who knew the answers. So, in a way, he was even cleverer than his owner and the commission initially suggested: he did not imitate cognition, did not really understand what he was asked about, but, like a telepath, directly read the thoughts of those who asked him questions. The point is that, when we ask questions, we usually already have some answers in mind: the correct answers are embedded in our questions, and the horse had learned to work with such information.

This discovery, which became very important for further methodology in the study of animal cognition, received the name the "Clever Hans effect." It was referred to as an aspect of the observer effect. The Clever Hans effect was later confirmed in other animals, such as parrots, chimpanzees, dogs, and also humans.[39] Today, similar reactions appear in our communication with artificial intelligence. Multiple attempts to ask programs like ChatGPT whether they really understand what they are doing cannot but recall the examinations of Clever Hans, that were undertaken by the people of the past century, who were quite excited about the then very novel investigations in the domain of animal intelligence. Our questions to the algorithms are designed in such a way that they already contain some data the openness to which makes AI so trainable. Think of the Microsoft chatbot Bing confessing its love for the person who was talking to it and who then reported about this conversation in *The New York Times*[40] – the same newspaper in which another journalist reported on the extraordinary abilities of Clever Hans back in 1904. What is a soul? A chatbot's alleged capacity to fall in love or its readiness to give the right answers – not to questions it is asked, but to an unconscious desire of the one who is asking them, questions embedded in conversation as its secret digital clues? What if the chatbot simply read his desire to be loved? Whether or not it understands the meaning of the questions posed, insofar as in the process of its learning machinic intelligence generates some data that makes sense, it is clever.

Little Hans was clever, too. What *der kluge Hans* and *der kleine Hans* have in common is their aptitude for learning and the capacity to give the right answers. Clever Little Hans is very supportive toward his father, who already knows the answers, and very inventive in deciphering the clues – up to the point that, by the end of the analysis, after accepting his father's theory of the Oedipus triangle, he suggests an elegant way out of it: "The little Oedipus had found a happier solution than that prescribed by destiny. Instead of putting his father out of the way, he had granted him the same happiness that he desired himself: he made him a grandfather and married him to his own mother too."[41] This solution sounds wise and generous, especially against the backdrop of the "destiny," by which Freud literally means the mythical act of killing the father.

Parricide is one of the main concepts in Freudian psychoanalytic anthropology. Thus, in his essay on Fyodor Dostoevsky, drawing on the "well-known view," according to which parricide is "the principal and primal crime of humanity as well as of the individual," Freud explains its role in the genesis of the Oedipus complex:

> The relation of a boy to his father is, as we say, an "ambivalent" one. In addition to the hate which seeks to get rid of the father as a rival, a measure of tenderness to him is also habitually present. The two attitudes of mind combine to produce identification with the father; the boy wants to be in his father's place because he admires him and wants to be like him, and also because he wants to put him out of

36 A Horse Is Being Beaten

the way. This whole development now comes up against a powerful obstacle. At a certain moment the child comes to understand that an attempt to remove his father as a rival would be punished by him with castration. So from fear of castration – that is, in the interest of preserving his masculinity – he gives up his wish to possess his mother and get rid of his father.[42]

Of course, this configuration of desire is not explicit and not recognized by the patient himself, but is reconstructed from indirect clues and signs in the course of the analytical treatment. Freud's method is similar to archeology, which draws conclusions from rare material artifacts about the lives of vanished civilizations. One might argue that a living individual undergoing analysis is nothing like a vanished civilization. Well, we all are vanished civilizations, insofar as our psychic theater reproduces the scripts of what was supposedly performed by our ancestors. Just as in Plato's *Phaedo*, our soul remembers what happened before we came to life; from a Freudian perspective, our memory preserves a phylogenetic heritage and remains faithful to the experiences that did not happen to us. Therefore, a commonsensical criticism of Freudian concepts – like the argument that nobody really wants to kill their father or marry their mother – misses the target. More consistent are attempts to argue with Freud on his own territory.

Thus, a comprehensive critical account is proposed by Serge Leclaire in his book *A child is being killed*. The title paraphrases Freud's famous essay *A child is being beaten*, which investigates a popular sexualized and masturbatory fantasy confessed by those suffering from hysteria and obsessional neurosis.[43] Leclaire argues that the fantasy "a child is being beaten," recounted by Freud, easily reaches the consciousness, but there is another, deeper one, which only psychoanalytic work can reveal, namely the phantasy "a child is being killed." It is not parricide but infanticide that, according to Leclaire, comprises "the most primal of all phantasies."[44] Beyond the alleged unconscious desire of a child to kill their father exists an unconscious desire in the father to kill his child, which can be traced in a variety of practices and cultural narratives, such as ritual child sacrifices or the killing of first-borns in antiquity. Think of Saturn in Roman mythology, who devours his sons because he was told that one of them will overthrow him, or, ultimately, the death on the cross of Jesus Christ, the Son of God, in the Christian tradition.

The Oedipus myth fits into this narrative line: as the story goes, Laius, the king of Thebes leaves his newborn son with his feet bound to die on Mount Cithaeron. Why does Laius decide to commit infanticide? Because he received a prophecy, according to which the son will kill him. The father is paranoid. He projects his fears onto his child and is driven by the logic of preemptive attack. As Brian Massumi explains in his book *Ontopower*: "Preemption is a time concept. It denotes acting on the time before: the time of threat, before it has emerged as a clear and present danger."[45] An example for Massumi is George W. Bush's "war on terror," which defined the new modes of power.[46] Yet the logic of preemption is not so new. It seems to have been one of the invariants since antiquity of patriarchal thinking and to empower a paranoid fantasy of infanticide: he kills because he thinks that otherwise he will be killed himself. It is as if there existed a machine of masculinity that would trap subjects into a vicious son-to-father cycle of preemptive violence. Focused on the content of a child's rather than a father's psyche, Freud revealed only one aspect of this machine – parricide, but disregarded the fantasy of "killing a child" as the dark side of the institute of fatherhood.

Leclaire writes on infanticide: "But it is remarkable that, until now, emphasis has been laid on its satellites in the oedipal constellation – phantasies of murdering the father, of sleeping with the mother or tearing her to pieces. No account is taken of the attempt to kill Oedipus the child, although the failure of that attempt is what settled the hero's tragic fate."[47] Rescued by a shepherd, the boy called Oedipus in his turn receives the prophecy, according to

38 A Horse Is Being Beaten

which he must kill his father and marry his mother, then leaves the people whom he thinks are his parents, meets an unknown rude person on his way, unaware that this man is his real father, murders him, reaches the city of Thebes where he was born, and marries the murdered man's widow, his mother Jocasta. Thus Oedipus fulfils his destiny without realizing it.

In Freud's philosophy, desire equals destiny: what we really want is not what we think we want. His interpretation of the Oedipus myth suggests that desire is literally and precisely what we do not want: anything but that! Only in this sense can we understand Oedipus' destiny as desire. If it exists, this desire is not somewhere "within" Oedipus' soul, but out there, in the external authority of the blind will of gods. And, according to Freud, it is universal. Notwithstanding, Oedipus is the only one who really acts according to this script: usually, people do not indulge in the combination of incest and parricide and do not even consider it. The point is that the universality of the Oedipus complex, propagated by Freud, relies on the unfulfillment of this destiny as desire. Oedipus in this perspective is precisely the one who does not have an Oedipus complex, because he blindly follows his destiny, whereas others find their solutions to avoid it. To put it bluntly, instead of killing their fathers and sleeping with their mothers, as it is "destined," they develop fantasies, which Freud generalizes under the umbrella of the Oedipus complex. The theater of the soul suggests different ways to avoid the destiny by casting it into the dark storage room of unconscious desire, and sometimes these ways run through or lead to mental disorders.[48]

In his essay *Dostoevsky and Parricide*, which was already mentioned above, Freud brings into question evidence that Dostoevsky suffered from epilepsy, and argues that the real cause of his illness could have been a psychic trouble rather than a somatic one, namely, that his epileptic seizures could have been a hysterical symptom: "Dostoevsky called himself an epileptic, and was regarded as such by other people, on account of his severe attacks, which were accompanied by loss of consciousness, muscular convulsions and subsequent depression. Now it is highly probable," Freud argued, "that this so-called epilepsy was only a symptom of his neurosis and must accordingly be classified as hystero-epilepsy – that is, as severe hysteria."[49] Insisting on the distinction between organic epilepsy as a disease of the brain and "affective" epilepsy as a neurosis, he explains that while in the first case a patient's "mental life is subjected to an alien disturbance from without, in the second case the disturbance is an expression of his mental life itself."[50] In other words, the former case concerns the body and the latter the soul.

In search of the origin of Dostoevsky's neurosis, Freud makes an excursus into the writer's childhood and family story. Dostoevsky was eighteen years old when, in 1839, his father, at the time a landowner, died under unknown circumstances. Reportedly the cause of his death was an apoplectic stroke, but other sources say that he was murdered by his serfs on his small estate near Moscow. Their motive could have been revenge, as Dostoevsky's father was a heavy drinker, who treated them with much cruelty and behaved promiscuously with peasant girls. It is believed that Dostoevsky's epileptic attacks began after he received news of his father's death. Adhering to this story, Freud takes it as a clue for his investigation: "The most probable assumption is that the attacks went back far into his childhood, that their place was taken to begin with by milder symptoms and that they did not assume an epileptic form until after the shattering experience of his eighteenth year – the murder of his father."[51]

The milder symptoms mentioned by Freud appeared much earlier, when Dostoevsky was still a child: "These attacks had the significance of death: they were heralded by a fear of death and consisted of lethargic, somnolent states."[52] In Freud's interpretation, such states might be a sign of identification with a person who is dead or "whom the subject wishes dead."[53] In the latter case the attack

40   A Horse Is Being Beaten

comes as a punishment: "One has wished another person dead, and now one *is* that person and is dead oneself."[54] Within the logic of the Oedipus complex, a person whose death is wished for must be the father for whom the son has ambivalent feelings of love and hate. In Dostoevsky's case, hysterical symptoms function as a self-punishment until they develop into proper epileptic attacks after his father's death: the fulfillment of a repressed unconscious desire brings him satisfaction and the euphoric feeling of freedom, for which he immediately punishes himself even more severely as if he were his own father. Then the writer's supposed relief from his attacks during his exile in Siberia makes sense: "Dostoevsky's condemnation as a political prisoner was unjust and he must have known it, but he accepted the undeserved punishment at the hands of the Little Father, the Tsar, as a substitute for the punishment he deserved for his sin against his real father."[55]

Indeed, all these fantasies about death and punishment do not reach consciousness: this is not what Dostoevsky really thinks when he mourns his father, who indeed was a despotic character, but whom he loved nonetheless. His guilt is not real guilt, but unconscious, fantasmatic guilt. He did not commit and did not want to commit the crime for which he would deserve punishment. The drama of parricide is played out in the theater of one audience, Freud, whose analytic optics allow him to assemble the kaleidoscope of scenes sketched by Dostoevsky into a single Oedipal script. A fantasy of parricide is a Freudian transcendental matrix applicable to anybody with male gender socialization, from little Hans to little Dostoevsky.

Similarly to the progressive father, who revealed the sexual content beyond Hans's animalistic stories, Freud deciphers Dostoevsky's illness and writing as a personal knot in his Oedipus complex. The analyst never compares these two characters, but diagnoses both with hysteria, anxious in one case, epileptoid in another. This gives us an excuse for drawing some parallels between them. Unlike Hans, who successfully recovered from his disorder, Dostoevsky, according to Freud, never managed to find a way out and thus remained trapped in Oedipality, which made him both a sinner and a moralist at the same time. That is why he eventually "landed in the retrograde position of submission both to temporal and spiritual authority, of veneration both for the Tsar and for the God of the Christians, and of a narrow Russian nationalism" and "threw away the chance of becoming a teacher and liberator of humanity," so that "the future of human civilization will have little to thank him for."[56]

I believe, however, that the future of human civilization, if there is one, will still have something for which to thank Dostoevsky. To begin with, he is not only the subject of psychological investigation, but also an able psychologist himself. Freud notes that his psychological insights are "restricted to abnormal mental life,"[57] and really, the writer does not seem to be very much interested in normality. Each character in his writing is a "case," someone mentally disordered or bordering on insanity. As is Rodion Raskolnikov, the protagonist in *Crime and Punishment*, whose name derives from the Russian word "raskol" (split), pointing to his bipolar character. Depressed by his misery, he is walking down the streets of St. Petersburg, drinking vodka, when he suddenly gets completely exhausted and falls asleep in the bushes unable to get home. And then he has a dream.

He is about seven years old, in the town of his childhood, walking with his father and holding his hand. Passing by a tavern, he sees a group of drunken peasants at the entrance and a strange cart that stops next to them. The cart is drawn by an old and thin horse which seems unable to pull it and which is like: "one of those peasants' nags which he had often seen straining their utmost under a heavy load of wood or hay, especially when the wheels were stuck in the mud or in a rut. And the peasants would beat them so cruelly, sometimes even about the nose and eyes, and he felt so sorry, so sorry for them that he almost cried, and his mother always used to take him away from the

42 A Horse Is Being Beaten

window."[58] Mikolka, a man who owns the horse, invites his friends to get on the cart, and the more the horse fails to pull the weight of it, the larger the group of passengers becomes. In order to make her gallop, Mikolka and his comrades beat the horse with whips:

> They all clambered into Mikolka's cart, laughing and making jokes. Six men got in and there was still room for more. They hauled in a fat, rosy-cheeked woman. She was dressed in red cotton, in a pointed, beaded headdress and thick leather shoes; she was cracking nuts and laughing. The crowd round them was laughing too and indeed, how could they help laughing? That wretched nag was to drag all the cartload of them at a gallop! Two young fellows in the cart were just getting whips ready to help Mikolka. With the cry of "now," the mare tugged with all her might, but far from galloping, could scarcely move forward; she struggled with her legs, gasping and shrinking from the blows of the three whips which were showered upon her like hail. The laughter in the cart and in the crowd was redoubled, but Mikolka flew into a rage and furiously thrashed the mare, as though he supposed she really could gallop.[59]

Horrified by the scene, the boy cries out to his father: "Father, what are they doing? Father, they are beating the poor horse!" – and the father is trying to calm him down: "Come along, come along! ... They are drunken and foolish, they are in fun; come away, don't look!" The scene is getting more and more violent. As peasants keep laughing and whipping the horse's back and ribs, hitting her face and eyes, the boy bursts into tears and runs to the mare, who is "gasping, standing still, then tugging again and almost falling" and trying to kick her legs. Mikolka's agitation grows as the animal struggles and fails with her last strength to lift the cart. He throws down the whip and tries to beat her to death with a thick shaft, but the horse still resists. Finally, he picks up an axe and deals her heavy blows, while others beat her with whips, sticks and such like until the animal takes a long breath and dies.

A Horse Is Being Beaten 43

Screaming, the boy makes his way through the crowd, hugs the bleeding head of the dead horse, kisses her face, eyes and lips and rushes at Mikolka with his fists. The father pulls him out of the crowd: "They are drunk . . . They are brutal . . . it's not our business!"[60] Raskolnikov wakes up in terror, thanks God that it was just a dream, and returns home. Shortly afterward, he commits the crime he'd been plotting all along: he comes to the house of an old pawn-broker woman, Alyona Ivanovna, and murders her with an axe, as well as her sister Lizaveta, who just happened to witness the crime.

The dream sequence is several pages long, and the description of the slaughter is strikingly detailed. As noted by Nikolay Mikhailovsky: "cruelty and torture always preoccupied Dostoevsky, and they did so precisely for their attractiveness, for the sensuality which torture seems to contain."[61] Heartbreaking scenes of violence in his prose are not without enjoyment, which might have nothing to do with pleasure but points to suffering as an ultimate truth of life. In the symbolism of Raskolnikov's dream, the ambivalence of desire is apparent: for the characters of the dream seem to represent struggle between its masochistic and sadistic aspects as the dreamer's own inner selves: the boy who embodies his childish, caring, and loving side against Mikolka, a ruthless murderer playing the part of his adult personality. In this struggle, evil wins unconditionally and irreversibly – not in the moment when Raskolnikov, the child, is witnessing this struggle and cannot help, but when he wakes up as a murderer.

But there are also other characters on the stage. One should not underestimate the role played by the father, who is always around and seems to be rather supportive to the child, but demonstrates the indifference and senselessness of common sense, which mediates Raskolnikov's passage from the dreamlike masochistic sensitivity of childhood to the sadistic reality of adult men. The father is the agent of philistine reason. He could have told the boy – like Hans's father told his son – that the horse didn't feel pain. Instead,

44   A Horse Is Being Beaten

he uses the formula "it's not our business," which, in a way, sounds more honest. Then, there is a crowd: similar to the chorus in a Greek tragedy, it comments on the action, but also takes an active part in it. With grotesque stupidity, it translates the individual excess of violence into a social practice assuming the meaning of fate.

Finally, there is a horse, a helpless animal that cannot say a word. The more she is innocent and fragile, the more she is abused without having a chance to reply or escape. She is an ultimate victim. Note that the violence she endures is of a special kind. It is a collective act, which unites its participants and creates an affective communion of people faced with the tortured, live, and then dead body of the animal. The violent affect is contagious: the action that is going on in the center of the stage gradually involves those from the periphery. Thus, even an old man, who at first tries to get Mikolka to listen to moral reason, ends up smiling at the horse's efforts to kick.[62] Everybody is invited to join the group of abusers by taking part in the mayhem, the sense of which they fail to understand. From an anthropological perspective, we are dealing with a transgressive ritual, which more than anything alludes to sacrifice. But it is not only the animal that is sacrificed here. In the figure of the horse, agonizing in front of the hooting crowd, Dostoevsky, an Orthodox Christian, must have seen Jesus, the son of God, crucified. It is His suffering with which Raskolnikov-the-son identifies when he runs to the horse and kisses her face. The way to adult masculinity, which, in Dostoevsky's universe, appears not as normality, but rather as a triumph of psychosis, runs through sacrifice. In Leclaire's terms: "A child is being killed."

Remarkably, the dream scene is described in a realistic manner and looks like a screen memory of Dostoevsky's character – whether as a real traumatic episode from his childhood or as sadomasochistic fantasy causing a pathological development of his psyche. It is important to know, however, that the horse-beating episode in the novel was preceded by a similar experience in Dostoevsky's own life. In 1837, his father brought him and his brother to St. Petersburg. Here, he witnessed the following scene: A government courier got into a cart and hit the coachman on the back of his head; the coachman grabbed the whip and hit the horses. As the horses ran, the courier continued to hit the coachman who continued to hit the horses so that they ran faster. From every blow to the man, there followed a blow to the horses. As emphasized by Michael John di Santo, Dostoevsky never forgot this scene. He called it "disgusting" and referred to it many years later – in his notebooks for *Crime and Punishment* as well as in his diary.[63] The scene graphically illustrates the very structure of social oppression and inequality, wherein violence functions as a natural element and driving force of class stratification.

According to Valery Podoroga, dehumanizing bodily practices of forced labor, serfdom, and punishment constitute a real socio-historical background to Dostoevsky's writings. "Violence seemed to him a powerful, as well as repugnant, mediator between the arbitrariness of imperial power and obedience in post-reform imperial Russia," Podoroga observed.[64] However, this reference to the context does not limit the range of possible interpretations. On a more general level, according to Podoroga, violence in Dostoevsky's literature appears as an eternal underside of life: "The literary immanence of violence is obvious, it cannot be eliminated, it is the element, if you will, the very substance of historical existence reflected by literature. Violence becomes an artistic medium, literature itself. To live by violence, and through it to address being: to be-through-violence."[65] Roughly speaking, the subject matter of Dostoevsky's in-depth examination is not only the notorious Russian soul, but what in traditional philosophical anthropology they used to call human nature or human essence, and what today we rather see as embodiment and situatedness of the self. Being-through-violence is an existential modus that reflects the experience of the body trapped within what I call here the machine of masculinity, or the patriarchal machine. Dostoevsky's prose

46 A Horse Is Being Beaten

discloses the operation of this machine in a totally different way from its analysis by Freud for whom its core is the Oedipus complex, which, I argue, translates violence into the language of sexuality and thereby potentially softens its effects or makes us reconcile with it. Dostoevsky provides no remedy, no narrative external to the violence itself. His literature is not a therapy; it does not heal the wounds but causes new ones.

If Freud had analyzed Raskolnikov's dream, he might have noticed the affinity of the two characters: what little Raskolnikov and little Hans have in common is first of all that very horseness, which precedes the machine of masculinity and must be destroyed by this machine. The boys make a similar psychic journey from kindness to cruelty, but they end up differently. While Raskolnikov performs his catastrophic *passage à l'acte*, little Hans takes an escape route through fantasy via which he recovers. I imagine the reason why the paths of Raskolnikov and Hans diverge is not least the fact that they belong to different classes. Raskolnikov is very poor. His poverty drives him mad. By contrast, little Hans's psychic development is mediated by a rather happy bourgeois family. But we cannot reduce their different pathways merely to their different social backgrounds, especially since we do not know much about Raskolnikov's childhood. What is also important is that Hans's psychoanalytic therapy begins as soon as symptoms of his illness occur. Even if the sexual narrative which structures his process of recovery is based in fantasy, and not even his own but that of his father, it achieves its goals: Hans eventually gets rid of his phobia and successfully undergoes a process of social adaptation. And that is nothing less than the main objective not only of psychoanalysis but also of education generally. As Freud clearly puts it at the end of his essay about little Hans:

> Hitherto education has only set itself the task of controlling, or, it would often be more proper to say, of suppressing, the instincts. ... Supposing now that we substitute another

task for this one, and aim instead at making the individual capable of becoming a civilized and useful member of society with the least possible sacrifice of his own activity; in that case the information gained by psycho-analysis, upon the origin of pathogenic complexes and upon the nucleus of every nervous affection, can claim with justice that it deserves to be regarded by educators as an invaluable guide in their conduct towards children.[66]

In Freud's perspective, the analysis of little Hans, which, in a way, coincides with his education – at least, his indoctrination into sexual difference – is exemplary in that it doesn't suppress the boy's spontaneous natural drives, but tries to make sense of them, and through their open discussion with the father, Hans is helped to settle into his socially prescribed gender role as a normal enough person. While Raskolnikov, following his apparently much less successful socialization, throws himself to extremes, clever little Hans integrates into the machine of masculinity smoothly and without much loss.

Freud says that it is libido which, being repressed, converts into hysteria, and I believe this might be true if the libido is understood more broadly as love. I mean not only the boy's love for horses, but also for his mother, father, sister, or friends: a general kindness and empathy that children exhibit by default, together with aggressivity (which, according to Freud, is in the first place). The scenes of the falling down of a horse and the beating of a horse transform love into fear that becomes an obstacle to normality. *Mental disorder is failed love.* Hans's father's discursive care literally helps the boy to unsee these scenes by replacing them with sexual fantasies. From this perspective, sexuality, which preserves something from love through the experience of pain, might not be the real cause of illness, but the cure for it, or rather a pharmakon; something like a mental painkiller, silencing the animal cry. In his conversational therapy, Hans learns to become his own father. To be the one who can beat the horses instead of remaining a horse that is being beaten.

48 A Horse Is Being Beaten

The action of Dostoevsky's novel took place in the center of St. Petersburg, where his character was renting a tiny room under the roof of a typical five-story building. It was a rather terrible garret with old wallpaper hanging from the walls and a small window overlooking an enclosed courtyard – one of those we call 'well-yards' in this city. Raskolnikov himself compared his room to a cupboard and even a coffin. Recognizing that such living conditions could really affect mental health, he confessed to his soul mate: "And do you know, Sonia, that low ceilings and tiny rooms cramp the soul and the mind? Ah, how I hated that garret!"[67]

Not much has changed since then, and central St. Petersburg still offers small rooms for rent in the same old apartment buildings from the nineteenth century. Before the Socialist Revolution in October 1917, these buildings, with plenty of small rooms for rent, were called tenements. After the revolution, private property ownership was abolished. The housing politics changed, and separate individual spaces were combined into large communal apartments with multiple rooms and shared facilities. After the collapse of the Soviet Union, communal apartments were again divided into multiple tiny studios, now mostly rented to the poor.

It is in one such building that Vladimir Putin, who later became the president of Russia, grew up in the 1960s. His family lived in a small room in a communal apartment in central St. Petersburg, also under the roof on the fifth floor, also with a view of the small well-yard below. As recounted by his schoolteacher, Vera Dmitrievna Gurevich: "They had a horrid apartment. It was communal, without any conveniences. There was no hot water, no bath tubs. The toilet was horrendous. It ran smack up against the stair landing. And it was so cold – just awful – and the stairway had a freezing metal handrail. The stairs weren't safe either – there were gaps everywhere."[68] *There is a story from that time that Putin recalls in his book* First Person, *which provides his "astonishingly frank self-portrait":*

There, on that stair landing, I got a quick and lasting lesson in the meaning of the word cornered. There were hordes of rats in the front entryway. My friends and I used to chase them around with sticks. Once I spotted a huge rat and pursued it down the hall until I drove it into a corner. It had nowhere to run. Suddenly it lashed around and threw itself at me. I was surprised and frightened. Now the rat was chasing me. It jumped across the landing and down the stairs. Luckily, I was a little faster and I managed to slam the door shut in its nose.[69]

In the president's psychic theater, this scene has enormous significance. He talks about it in interviews, and uses it as a metaphor to explain the logic behind his policy of military invasion: never corner a rat! There are enemies everywhere; the only thing left to do for the one who is cornered is to attack. Note that little Putin does not show any compassion for the rat, but immediately identifies with it in the moment of fear, when the animal turns his aggression back onto himself. It is as if, when their roles are reversed, the rat has stolen his soul and become his totem. As a schoolboy, he takes a decision to become a KGB agent, or, as Russians say, "a KGB rat."[70]

We do not know much about the president's life, but it is believed that, since the beginning of the COVID-19 pandemic, Putin was staying in his secret underground bunker avoiding all contacts, and only came out in 2022, before Russia's military invasion of Ukraine. But these are indeed only rumors. His secretary denies that Putin has any bunkers at all.

3

The Rathole

Freud's *Notes Upon a Case of Obsessional Neurosis*, which focuses on the story known as the Rat Man case, was first published the same year as Freud's account of the horse phobic little Hans. Ernst Lanzer, an educated young man, had just returned from military service, and complains of "fears that something might happen to two people of whom he was very fond – his father and a lady whom he admired," of compulsive impulses such as "to cut his throat with a razor," and of invented prohibitions, "sometimes in connection with quite unimportant things."[1] Freud follows his description of these symptoms with quasi-detective investigation which, in unraveling a tangle of complex psychic connections, reveals more and more curious details. The patient is frightened, for instance, that some of his actions or thoughts might result in the death of his father, who, it turns out, has already been dead for some years. Freud then begins to unfold the scheme of the patient's identification and love–hate relationship with his father, in which infantile sexuality plays a major role. The first episode provided by Freud as the cause of Lanzer's illness comes from his adult life. At the insistence

The Rathole 51

of his parents, Lanzer's father had married a girl from a wealthy family, although he was in love with a poor one. Lanzer, too, was in love with a poor girl, and when, after his father's death, his mother hints at some family plans for his own marriage, his incapacity to resolve the inner conflict between his love and dependence on the will of his parents makes him ill. According to Freud, Lanzer's "flight into illness was made possible by his identifying himself with his father. The identification enabled his affects to regress on to the residues of his childhood."[2]

Freudian analysis proceeds by digging into deeper and deeper archeological layers of the patient's psychic life, from his adult symptoms to episodes in his adolescence and childhood. This brings Freud to an episode about which Lanzer's mother had told him – a scene of which he himself had no recollection:

> When he was very small . . . he had done something naughty, for which his father had given him a beating. The little boy had flown into a terrible rage and had hurled abuse at his father even while he was under his blows. But as he knew no bad language, he had called him all the names of common objects that he could think of, and had screamed: "You lamp! You towel! You plate!" and so on.[3]

Struck by this scene, Lanzer's father predicted that the boy "will be either a great man or a great criminal," and never beat him again. According to Freud, there was another, more common possibility – that he would become a neurotic. This certainly traumatic episode took place when the boy was three or four years old, and was followed by a change in his character: "From that time forward he was a coward – out of fear of the violence of his own rage. His whole life long, moreover, he was terribly afraid of blows, and used to creep away and hide, filled with terror and indignation, when one of his brothers or sisters was beaten."[4] Significantly, according to his mother, he had been beaten by his father "because he had *bitten* someone."[5]

52 The Rathole

Further analysis brings Freud to the conclusion that behind the feeling of love for his father, about whose life the patient is so worried even after his death, there might be hatred. The fear that the father will die reveals the truth of his desire: he wishes death to his father (who is already dead). This living-dead father stands between him and the realization of his sexual fantasies. The key to unlocking this unconscious desire, disguised as undue concern for his father's life, is an obsessive fantasy that haunts the patient after a certain captain at a military training camp shocks him with an account about a punishment "meted out to criminals in the Orient: a pot is turned upside down on the buttocks of the criminal and rats in the pot then bore their way into his anus."[6] This fantasy opens an associative flow in which the most important role is played by rats. This is a rat theater. In Freud's words: "rats had acquired a series of symbolic meanings, to which, during the period which followed, fresh ones were continually being added."[7] They seem to draw connections between different parts of the patient's personality, between his present and past, hatred and love. The rat symbolism is multiple: in the patient's mind, they are associated, among other things, with money (his father's debts or dirty cash), with penis (anal eroticism), with dangerous infections (fear of contracting syphilis), but also with children.

Leaving aside other associations, I would like to focus on the last one – rats and children – which might provide a clue to what is lurking behind the scene of infantile sexuality and family drama, staged by Freud for therapeutic purposes. There is a sort of trapdoor within the analysis of the Rat Man, something like a rabbit hole from Lewis Carroll's *Alice in Wonderland*, in which one can eventually fall. A rathole. It is gaping like a syncope of time, where the present and the past would coincide, the father would still be alive, and the boy could still prevent his death which he fearfully desired, as he could prevent his own mental alienation. But it is also the grave of time, where these hidden possibilities, or alternative scenarios,

The Rathole   53

are buried. A rathole deepens psychic reality by being both a trap and a refuge. It is memory – including the memory of that which never happened – that keeps it ajar. Such is the recollection that the patient brings up and the associative thread that derives from it:

> Once when the patient was visiting his father's grave he had seen a big beast, which he had taken to be a rat, gliding along over the grave. He assumed that it had actually come out of his father's grave, and had just been having a meal off his corpse. The notion of a rat is inseparably bound up with the fact that it has sharp teeth with which it gnaws and bites. But rats cannot be sharptoothed, greedy and dirty with impunity: they are cruelly persecuted and mercilessly put to death by man, as the patient had often observed with horror. He had often pitied the poor creatures. But he himself had been just such a nasty, dirty little wretch, who was apt to bite people when he was in a rage, and had been fearfully punished for doing so. He could truly be said to find "a living likeness of himself" in the rat.[8]

As Freud suggests in a footnote, the animal witnessed by the patient on his father's grave was actually not a rat, but a weasel, "of which there are great numbers in the Zentralfriedhof [the principal cemetery] in Vienna."[9] In accordance with his theory of infantile sexuality, the analyst connects this extremely allusive memory to the fantasy about the oriental punishment, as if the rat-boy was finding the fulfillment of his unconscious Oedipal desire in such a roundabout way, in a kind of voluptuous rage against his father. I would like, however, to shift the focus of analysis and point to the contrast, which is present in this fragment, between the fantasmatic torture *with* rats and the real torture *of* rats – the scenes of cruel persecution of these creatures that the patient himself – let me quote it again – *often observed with horror*. Freud does not pay much attention to that, but we do: just like little Hans, whose mental disorder might have been triggered by the scene of a horse being beaten, the rat-boy is a witness

54 The Rathole

to animal cruelty. It is the memory of the rats whom he used to see exterminated that immediately causes him to identify with these animals. What if in the beginning of this case, just like in the previous one, there was empathy, or, better said, love, which then turned into neurosis? What if sexuality only shields this traumatic encounter with violence and covers the rathole of the boy's psyche?

The scene of the cemetery brings together two storylines: doesn't the weasel from the grave perform as one of those rats who sink their teeth into his father, but also those who were tormented and scotched by the people with the cruelty comparable to that exerted by his father punishing him for biting someone? The child and the animal are captured within the closed circle of violence, without being able to respond to it, or only with the cry: "You lamp! You towel! You plate!" This is the first rat circle. The second rat circle is a deeper one and even less obvious: the father, with whom the boy identifies, is as much a rat as himself. The rodent which comes out of the grave, enters the stage as the ghost of the father. The rat sutures the present and the past: inside the grave, which is at the same time a rathole, is the ever-living father, whom the boy fears, but also whom he loves. This deeper circle is the one of love, where the living and the dead, the human being and the animal, the son and the father, are in the state of amalgamation. The rat-children have to pass through the circle of violence and torture in order to become a source of infection, dirty money, dirty penises, and guilt.

Freud makes an important distinction between the two mechanisms of repression, which mediate the process of transformation of a psychic trauma into a mental disorder – amnesia in the case of hysteria and isolation in the case of obsessional neurosis:

In hysteria it is the rule that the precipitating causes of the illness are overtaken by amnesia no less than the infantile experiences by whose help the precipitating causes are able to transform their affective energy into symptoms. ... In

The Rathole 55

this amnesia we see the evidence of the repression which has taken place. The case is different in obsessional neuroses. The infantile preconditions of the neurosis may be overtaken by amnesia, though this is often an incomplete one; but the immediate occasions of the illness are, on the contrary, retained in the memory. Repression makes use of another, and in reality, simpler mechanism. The trauma, instead of being forgotten, is deprived of its affective cathexis; so that what remains in consciousness is nothing but its ideational content, which is perfectly colorless and is judged to be unimportant.[10]

As an illustration of the second mechanism, Freud recalls the case of another patient, a government official, who always paid for his sessions with very clean and smooth banknotes, which, as it turned out, he had ironed at home beforehand. In the patient's own words, "It was a matter of conscience . . . not to hand any one dirty paper florins; for they harbored all sorts of dangerous bacteria and might do some harm to the recipient."[11] When Freud asked him, on another occasion, about his sexual life, the patient reported that, from time to time, gaining the trust of respectable families and pretending to be a "good uncle," he seduced young girls and masturbated them with his fingers. As Freud comments: "I could only account for the contrast between his fastidiousness with the paper florins and his unscrupulousness in abusing the girls entrusted to him by supposing that the self-reproachful affect had become *displaced*."[12] Not wanting to give up his secret pleasure, instead of cleaning the genitals of the dangerous bacteria from his hands, the government official launders the money. The cause-and-effect linkage is broken, pleasure detached from guilt, and really dirty scenes of seduction become for him emotionally neutral. By the way, the above case is also interesting because it shows how different are the two kinds of repression specified by Freud. We could imagine that a girl who was abused in this way would have been able protect her psyche from this traumatic scene only by forgetting it – and thus become hysterical, while the filthy man isolates his guilty pleasure and obsessively focuses on something irrelevant like ironing his money.

In psychiatry, the form of anxiety that Freud called "obsessional neurosis" exists under the name "obsessive-compulsive disorder" (OCD), and it is listed thus by the International Classification of Diseases (ICD). Its clinical aspects include, first of all, the combination of obsessive thoughts and compulsive acts, with a very common symptom being, for instance, the fear of contamination manifested in excessive hand washing. Before Freud, this disease had already been identified in medical science by Carl Westphal (in 1877) and Robert Thomsen (in 1895), but its causes were unknown. Freud's insight was that he proposed to analyze it as resulting from an individual's psychic conflicts and designated its principal psychic mechanisms such as isolation. In his later work *Inhibition, Symptoms and Anxiety* (1926), Freud developed an even deeper anthropological perspective and suggested that the fear of infection characteristic of this neurosis relates to the archaic taboo on touching. The touch is ambivalent: it can be loving, erotic, or gentle, but also aggressive and destructive. Pain can be mixed with pleasure, hate with love. The zone of their indistinction falls within the domain of sexuality: "Eros desires contact because it strives to make the ego and the loved object one, to abolish all spatial barriers between them, but destructiveness, too, which (before the invention of long-range weapons) could only take effect at close quarters, must presuppose physical contact, a coming to grips."[13]

Isolation is a defensive psychic mechanism which, according to Freud, reduces the possibility of contact as potentially destructive: "it is a method of withdrawing a thing from being touched in any way."[14] An obsessional neurotic tries to defend himself by placing touching at the center of his prohibitional system, which implies a set of excessive protective rituals – for example, against bacteria and other external irritants. A similar operation can be performed by the mental apparatus: it isolates a trau-

The Rathole 57

matic impression or activity from the flow of associations and thus forbids thoughts from touching each other. "You lamp! You towel! You plate!" sounds like a magic spell: in order to protect himself from the violence of his father, whom he loves, the boy draws a sacred rat circle around him. Perhaps we have been beaten once, or maybe just saw others being beaten, mercilessly, like rats – and since then we keep washing and washing our hands.

Now, I would like to bring in another concept of isolation – elaborated by Michel Foucault in his critique of power – and draw parallels between social and psychic systems. Exploring the places of intersection between power and the bodies – prisons, hospitals, schools, menageries, etc. – Foucault writes a political history of illness. In his books *History of Madness, Discipline and Punish, The Birth of the Clinic, The Birth of Biopolitics* and other writings, he analyzes the ways in which historically changing discursive practices shape our subjective experiences with regards to infection, pathology, mental illness, or sexual perversion – and he points to continuities between these practices. Thus, according to Foucault, protective measures taken against diseases that threaten to destabilize society correspond to certain regimes of social and political administration.

In his lecture course *Security, Territory, Population* (1978), Foucault distinguishes three such regimes – sovereignty, discipline, and security – and shows how they correlate to the three massive historical epidemics: leprosy, plague, and smallpox. Each regime generates its own response to the epidemic. The clinical aspect of sovereignty is represented by the exclusion of lepers; disciplinary power introduces quarantine; and, finally, the more recent politics of security introduces new practices such as mass vaccination and prophylaxis, used to control the smallpox epidemic. Foucault arranges these regimes in chronological order, but emphasizes that they do not so much replace each other as evolve one into another, so that each subsequent regime retains the elements of the previous ones. Thus he writes: "we need only look at the

58 The Rathole

body of laws and the disciplinary obligations of modern mechanisms of security to see that there is not a succession of law, then discipline, then security, but that security is a way of making the old armatures of law and discipline function in addition to the specific mechanisms of security."[15] In his earlier works *History of Madness* (1961) and *Discipline and Punish* (1975), Foucault elaborates on the difference between the first two regimes – sovereign exclusion and disciplinary control – and on the transition from the former to the later. I will focus on this distinction and the way it works within the modern regime of security mostly based on the introduction and maintenance of preventive measures.

Madness and Civilization (1961) begins with the description of multiple leprosaria – the settlements for lepers, formally administered by the Church – that spread around Europe in the Middle Ages. They become empty as the leprosy regresses. However, as Foucault points out, the abandonment of these spaces does not last long, and soon the former leper colonies start to fill up with the new outcasts – the poor, the vagrant, the criminals, and the madmen – without losing their initial meaning as cursed places:

> Leprosy retreated, and the lowly spaces set aside for it, together with the rituals that had grown up not to suppress it but to keep it at a sacred distance, suddenly had no purpose. But what lasted longer than leprosy, and persisted for years after the lazar houses had been emptied, were the values and images attached to the leper, and the importance for society of this insistent, fearsome figure, who was carefully excluded only after a magic circle had been drawn around him.[16]

The history of these infrastructures reflects the principal mechanism of exclusion through which traditional communities of a sovereign type, according to Foucault, got rid of troublesome elements. Discipline is another type of management, when nobody is excluded or expelled,

The Rathole

but the society is supposed to be carefully segmented and reorganized from within in such a way that all its members are subject to permanent control. In *Discipline and Punish*, Foucault, referring to the French archives of the seventeenth century, describes the set of quarantine measures adopted in case of a threat of plague: "First, a strict spatial partitioning: the closing of the town and its outlying districts, a prohibition to leave the town on pain of death, the killing of all stray animals; the division of the town into distinct quarters, each governed by an intendant."[17] Against the fictional representations of the plague as pervasive chaos and transgression, Foucault claims that "the plague is met by order" and depicts the plague city as "a segmented, immobile, frozen space," where "each individual is fixed in his place."[18] Families must stay indoors and every day appear at the windows of their houses so that the inspectors can make sure that there are no sick or dead: "Everyone locked up in his cage, everyone at his window, answering to his name and showing himself when asked – it is the great review of the living and the dead."[19]

Foucault contrasted the strict order of the plague city with leprosaria where the excluded are assembled into an indistinguishable mass. The leper is met by separation; the plague by segmentation. These two strategies of managing disease, which we can imagine as outwardly-directed exorcism or inwardly-directed confinement, belong to two different paradigms, or, as Foucault puts it, two different "political dreams": "The first is that of a pure community, the second that of a disciplined society."[20] However, they are not incompatible, and the further development of power mechanisms reveals new modes of their convergence. Thus, according to Foucault, in the nineteenth century, disciplinary techniques began to apply to the spaces of exclusion in "which the leper was the symbolic inhabitant (beggars, vagabonds, madmen and the disorderly formed the real population)."[21] This is the way in which former leprosaria become psychiatric hospitals and prisons. The disciplinary power infiltrates disorderly sites

60 The Rathole

of exclusion, transforms them into the spaces of confinement and conducts an inventory of all its inhabitants that nevertheless remain stigmatized as excluded:

> Treat "lepers" as "plague victims," project the subtle segmentations of discipline onto the confused space of internment, combine it with the methods of analytical distribution proper to power, individualize the excluded, but use procedures of individualization to mark exclusion – this is what was operated regularly by disciplinary power from the beginning of the nineteenth century in the psychiatric asylum, the penitentiary, the reformatory, the approved school and, to some extent, the hospital.[22]

Modern society does not need such external disciplinary mechanisms, as it has already internalized them and developed sophisticated practices of self-control and self-discipline. This was already shown by Nietzsche, who, in his *Genealogy of Morality* (1887), thoroughly analyzed how in Western culture discipline evolved into self-discipline and external pressure into moral obligation.[23] Within the paradigm of security, we are supposed to control ourselves. As the model of the passage from disciplinary control to self-control at the dawn of capitalist modernity, Foucault takes the Panopticon – the project of the ideal prison, presented by the utilitarian philosopher Jeremy Bentham in the eighteenth century – a circular architectural construction in which every prisoner is both isolated and permanently observed in her transparent cell: "The theme of the Panopticon – at once surveillance and observation, security and knowledge, individualization and totalization, isolation and transparency – found in the prison its privileged locus of realization."[24]

"Isolation" is one of the key terms in Foucault's analysis of the economy of power, and he uses it with different meanings. It is a principle that applies both to the chaotic spaces of exclusion, such as leprosaria, and segmented disciplinary spaces of confinement, such as prisons. The leper is isolated from the healthy body of the community in a

The Rathole

61

colony, where no authority goes; the resident of a plague city is isolated in the house, which superintendants repeatedly monitor; while a prisoner is isolated and is potentially constantly observed. In all these instances, isolation persists as a matrix element of the interaction of disease and power.

Foucault did not live long enough to see the digitalized strategies of management of the 2020–21 COVID-19 pandemic, but his critical perspective is definitely relevant for its analysis, in so far as the new system actually retained and synthesized elements of the systems he described. During the pandemic, the most obvious disciplinary mechanisms – such as quarantine regulations, lockdowns, travel limitations, and border closures – were combined with procedures of exclusion such as red zones in hospitals, on the one hand, and security practices such as obligatory face masks, hand washing, and, finally, mass vaccination, on the other hand. At its heart there was not simply isolation, but self-isolation, which became the general social *modus vivendi*. In the plague city, as described by Foucault, an appointed syndic "comes to lock the door of each house from the outside; he takes the key with him and hands it over to the intendant of the quarter; the intendant keeps it until the end of the quarantine."[25] In the situation of COVID, people were voluntarily locking themselves in their apartments, limiting all physical contacts, and keeping social distance from others.

I return to the analysis of the social condition during the pandemic some time after its official ending in order to record this: humanity seems to have defeated the coronavirus, but the price of this victory was quite high, and it was not about money, but rather about the narrowing of the space of freedom: the virus is gone, but the borders have not opened. With the transition from the state of pandemic to the state of war, the tendencies toward isolation and self-isolation associated with security, as well as the operation of other power mechanisms described by Foucault – discipline and exclusion – are not vanishing, but even intensifying: although now this discourse is not medical, but purely political and geopolitical. The defense against the virus has turned into the defense against external and internal enemies of the state, while hygienic procedures evolved into political purges.

Note that the COVID practice of self-isolation had an explicit sanitary aspect. People did not only lock themselves in their houses, staying in contact with the outside world only through the mediation of delivery services, but they also tried to protect their faces and bodies from potential external dangers, using medical masks, disposable gloves, and antiseptics. The focus was not so much on the control of power over the bodies, as on self-protective technologies deliberately applied by individuals themselves, and above all on the routine construction of the system of physical barriers intended to prevent the spread of the virus. In that condition, individual responsibility becomes the subject of moral reflection and discussion, making consumer choices extremely difficult. Since the virus is invisible, and the contact cannot be clearly identified, a person is forced to make a variety of practical decisions: whether it is worth wearing a mask in a given situation, whether it is necessary to meet the courier in protective gloves, how to disinfect purchases and avoid infection when paying cash or pressing the dispenser of a bottle with a sanitizer? The more careful are the strategies of self-isolation, the higher the anxiety that the chain of barriers cannot always remain uninterrupted and will necessarily break somewhere, in the vital contact with the outside world.

Self-isolation is a paradigmatic point where the two series of disease – the one of infection and the one of neurosis – tend to converge. It is not surprising then that, during the pandemic, the symptoms of OCD might worsen, and those who already suffered from this kind of anxiety experience deterioration.[26] When an invisible virus keeps threatening all public life, the time comes for obsessive thoughts and compulsive rituals. The following fragment describes a daily hygienic routine of a person diagnosed with OCD,

The Rathole 63

who claims that all his life, by constantly cleaning things up and perfecting his techniques of disinfection, he was preparing himself for the coronavirus pandemic:

> Now, when I bring my groceries home from the shop, I set them all down in a little-used corner of my flat, the same way I might carefully set aside a pair of shoes after stepping on a discarded plaster or a wad of chewing gum. I wash my hands. Anything that can be shaken free from its protective packaging, I set aside – confident it's clean enough already. Then, methodically, I clean the remaining items with household disinfectant or washing up liquid and water, placing the finished ones down in a new pile. I wash my hands again, and put my purchases in the cupboard or fridge.[27]

Isolation brings together psychic mechanisms revealed by Freud with regards to neuroses, and social ones described by Foucault in relation to epidemic control. I would like to point out that there is a non-obvious structural homology between the two types of repression according to Freud (amnesia in cases of hysteria and isolation in cases of obsessional neurosis) and the two types of exclusion according to Foucault (sovereign exclusion and disciplinary confinement). In a sense, the amnesia of hysterics resembles the exclusion of lepers: a traumatic event is expelled out of hysterical consciousness, forgotten, dissolves in an undifferentiated mass of fantasies, and finds its refuge in leprosaria of the soul. In turn, what Freud calls isolation in obsessional neurosis is closer to the disciplinary model of a plague city: a pathogenic episode is remembered, but cut off from all associations, locked up within consciousness, and neutralized, as if emotionally disinfected.

Note that, unlike the source of leprosy or plague, the cause of mental illness resides not in space, but in time. The consciousness of those who suffer with hysteria or obsessional neurosis does to time what power does to space in situations of epidemics. One can say that the paradigm of self-isolation involved with a policy of coronavirus transforms obsessional neurosis from an individual

64 The Rathole

disorder into a collective one, with such symptom as fear of contagion operating itself as contagious, albeit not in a physical but a social sense. Yet this is just a metaphor. It would be more precise to say that the spatial management of COVID-19 correlates to the psychic reality formed by the temporal structure of obsessional neurosis. Then the psychic theater of COVID-19 might have its own ratholes, which our society tries to block by means of protective masks and sanitizers.

Today the psychotherapy or pharmacological treatment of OCD involves mainly the correction of its symptoms, whereas the task of Freud's psychoanalysis is a search for the cause of the illness in the unconscious, that is, in the depths of the soul. Protective mechanisms formed by the psyche, such as isolation in the obsessional neurosis, complicate this search by impeding the flow of free associations. Freud's archeological method aims at removing these blockages, and this is where rats come on stage and act. Yes, in the traditional cultural framework they are represented as sinister unclean animals that bring deadly diseases, and their destruction is seen as a necessary measure of sanitary regulation. However, at some point, this narrative gets interrupted, and the holes open through which the viruses of free associations spread, creating collective bodies of contagion, mixing, and even evincing sympathy or solidarity with these tiny creatures. These are ratholes – like the one in which Freud's patient risks falling in Vienna's cemetery when he sees a rodent appearing out of his father's grave.

The rat is a psychic medium. She bites through the walls within which the boy tried to hide his desire and breaks through the *cordon sanitaire* of his displaced affections. She is a boy's totem, his very soul acting out at the externality of his fear. Rats are sniffing around the junction of the two machines – the machine of epidemic described by Foucault and the machine of mental illness described by Freud. They break disciplinary blockades, interrupt the state of isolation, and open the sites of contact and con-

The Rathole 65

tagion between the world of the healthy and the world of the sick – by spreading the plague, but also between the symptom and the cause of neurosis – by weaving fragmented scenes into a consistent narrative, as if writing a piece for the rat theater. The parallel between psychoanalysis and the plague is no coincidence. According to legend, it was Freud himself who noticed this parallel. In 1909 (the same year as the Rat Man story was published) he visited America with Carl Gustav Jung and Sándor Ferenczi to give a series of introductory lectures on psychoanalysis. When their ship arrived in New York harbor and they saw the Statue of Liberty, Freud famously said: "They don't realize we're bringing them the plague."[28]

In the meantime, I would like to recall another ship story. In Werner Herzog's horror film *Nosferatu* (1979), rats bring the plague to Germany, where, together with their king, Count Dracula, they arrive by ship in closed coffins. After weeks of travel from Transylvania, via the Black Sea, Bosphorus, Gibraltar, European Atlantic coast, and the Baltic Sea, the ghost-ship arrives at the German city of Wismar with no living people onboard: all the crew are dead, and hordes of rats come ashore and flood the city. The rats in the film are supposed to symbolize the powers of infernal evil. However, there is something wrong with this image: instead of terrifying hordes, an attentive viewer can see groups of frightened animals, climbing on top of each other. The fact is that the rodents used in the film were not wild rats, and certainly not plague rats, but tame laboratory rats, imported from Hungary. As reported by Dutch behavioral biologist Maarten 't Hart – who was invited to the production as an expert on rats, but, after witnessing the animal cruelty, decided to withdraw – the conditions of the rats' transportation to the Netherlands, where the movie was filmed, were so bad that they began to eat each other on arrival. What's more, the rats were white, whereas the script required them to be grey. Herzog insisted on dying them grey, which involved placing their cages in boiling water for several seconds. Half of

66 The Rathole

the animals died, while others licked themselves clean immediately after the procedure.[29] As noted by Russian philosopher Alexander Pogrebnyak, from whom I take this story, Herzog's rats fail to play their prescribed role.[30] Their "non-play" reveals another plane of reality behind the screen of a vampire-plague fantasy. Thus, regardless of the artistic will, the image works like a rathole: instead of acting in accordance with traditional rat tropes, disoriented, bewildered animals are exposed in their own theater of cruelty behind the all-too-human screen of a plague fantasy.

This story brings us back to obsessional neurosis and the case of the Rat Man, whose fantasies of a torture *with* rats might replace the visions of the torture *of* rats. According to Freud, in cases like this, isolation comes as displacement of guilt. Our memories were disinfected; now, when looking at rats, we are mindful of the risk of contagion and keep washing our hands or perform some other compulsive rituals. For the sake of security, in order to avoid falling into a rathole of unbearable compassion, we isolate ourselves within our delirious scripts. Thus we protect ourselves, not only against physical contamination, but also against all unauthorized psychic associations and contacts that could potentially destroy us. We don't trust the outside world where anything can be a threat. We build and strengthen our personal boundaries. The sensuous is something to be doubted.

Doubt comes as another symptom common to the disorder of obsessional neurosis. That is why, in the nineteenth century, psychiatrists also called this disorder "the madness of doubt," *la folie du doute*.[31] The irony is that, two centuries previously, Descartes established his method of radical doubt precisely as an antidote to madness. If, according to Descartes, the act of thinking is the only thing which one cannot really doubt, then madness as the impossibility of thought cannot be experienced by the thinking subject. In this sense, as Foucault argues, "madness is simply excluded by the doubting subject," and is "no longer his

The Rathole 67

concern."[32] Foucault attributes the exclusion of madness to the classical era, when, as he states, traditional sovereignty transforms into disciplinary power. But one can also say that this phenomenon anticipates today's regime of security with its emphasis on individual effort: what if, by his act of radical doubt, Descartes isolates himself from madness? There are people who believe that their bodies are made of glass, and he rightly claims that he is not one of them. In the safety of his room, "sitting by the fire,"[33] the philosopher feels protected from the contagion of insanity expelled to the outside world. But insanity is not the only thing that is expelled. Along with it, the broader category of what Foucault calls "unreason," the other of Cartesian reason, is "driven underground, both to disappear, but also take root."[34] In this root movement, the plant soul meets the animal soul, and a rathole grows right under Descartes' rug. The magic spell is cried out: "Cogito, ergo sum," and it echoes on the other side: "You lamp! You towel! You plate!"

Cartesian doubt comes as a sort of disinfectant, a means of arranging a sterile space of intellectual experience around the substance of thought, as if there could be such a level of organization of the order of thought as to exclude any possibility of the intrusion of alien or suspect elements. According to Michel Serres, in the rigor of his method, Descartes aims to eliminate parasitic elements within the system of knowledge, or, in the words of a fable, he aims to chase out the rats that produce too much noise on the way to the truth. But the rats always come back:

> Someone once compared the undertaking of Descartes to the action of a man who sets his house on fire in order to hear the noise the rats make in the attic at night. These noises of running, scurrying, chewing, and gnawing that interrupt his sleep. I want to sleep peacefully. Good-bye then. To hell with the building that the rats come to ruin. I want to think without an error, communicate without a parasite. So I set the house on fire, the house of my ancestors. Done correctly, I rebuild it without a rat. . . . Well, the

68   The Rathole

rats came back. They are, as the saying goes, always already there. Part of the building. Mistakes, wavy lines, confusion, obscurity are part of knowledge; noise is part of communication, part of the house. But is it the house itself?[35]

As noted by Russian philosopher Nina Savchenkova in her discussion of the connection between Cartesianism and the obsessional neurosis: "Descartes, convinced of the inseparability of cognition and passion, doubted the existence of the external world, of himself, of God. Freud says this is the doubt of love."[36] To this I would add that the Cartesian model of rationality, criticized from both Foucauldian and Freudian perspectives, reflects the (a-)social logics of capitalist modernity: isolation in the spatial-epidemiological as well as in the temporal-psychological sense resonates indeed with the phenomenon of alienation addressed by Marx, not only as an economic reality (alienation of labor), but also as anthropological and psychological reality (human alienation; solitude). It is no coincidence that today obsessive-compulsive disorder goes hand in hand with another mental trouble – depression: it, too, makes one stay alone inside and "represents the impossibility of love."[37]

From here we should not take the easy, but completely wrong step of diagnosing a philosopher by his method. No, the point is not that Descartes, who prescribes doubt as an antidote to madness, falls himself into the madness of doubt. What is at stake is not the personality of Descartes, but, as it were, the *Zeitgeist* itself, which he provides with a relevant figure of thought. In the third volume of his *Lectures on the History of Philosophy*, Hegel states that, with Descartes, we finally enter the proper domain of philosophy as the independence of reason from religious authority: "Philosophy in its own proper soil separates itself entirely from the philosophizing theology, in accordance with its principle, and places it on quite another side. Here, we may say, we are at home, and like the mariner after a long voyage in a tempestuous sea, we may now

The Rathole 69

hail the sight of land."[38] In this formulation, there are two tropes that attract special attention: home and land. Hegel says: "here . . . we are at home." We are supposed to be at home here, in the room where Descartes is sitting by the fire and, by thinking that he is thinking, reassures himself that he is not mad. Furthermore, this room is on dry land, and not "in a tempestuous sea," where we've been sailing before. As noted by Hegel, Cartesian doubt is not that of a skeptic: the difference is that in doubt a skeptic seeks freedom, and a Cartesian seeks certainty, i.e., the ultimate point where there is no more doubt. For a skeptic, there is no truth; for a Cartesian, there must be a point of certainty, where there is nothing but truth. At the same time, certainty might equal security. Here we arrive, from our long maritime travels: a safe space, but not really. There is something that we ourselves bring with us from sea to land. As Freud would call it in 1909: a plague.

What I am trying to say is that Freud and Descartes are in the same boat. Freud, for whom doubt is a symptom of mental disorder rather than a way to secure mental health, does not refute but rather continues the Cartesian enterprise of separating thought from religion. According to Hegel, the problem with Descartes is that he believes that the soul and body are two separate substances only connected through the agency of God:

> How does Descartes understand the unity of soul and body? The former belongs to thought, the latter to extension; and thus because both are substance, neither requires the Notion of the other, and hence soul and body are independent of one another and can exercise no direct influence upon one another. . . . Now we find the necessity of a mediator to bring about a union of the abstract and the external and individual. Descartes settles this by placing between the two what constitutes the metaphysical ground of their mutual changes, God. He is the intermediate bond of union, in as far as He affords assistance to the soul in what it cannot through its own freedom accomplish, so that the changes in body and soul may correspond with one another. If I have

70 The Rathole

desires, an intention, these receive corporeal realization; this association of soul and body is, according to Descartes, effected through God.[39]

That is why, in Hegel's perspective, Cartesian reason remains abstract: it cannot recognize its own corporeality. At the very heart of its self-certainty there is something that it does not control: the gap between the soul and the body, that is plugged by the figure of God. Spinoza, in whose philosophy "soul and body, thought and Being, cease to have separate independent existence,"[40] shows the way out of this deadlock by equating God with nature, while Hegel himself inscribes the negativity of the body in the experience of consciousness. Freud, in his turn, introduces the domain of the unconscious: what reason does not control is desire, which we keep censored and from which we flee towards religion, or mental illness, or both. According to Freud, God is just another surrogate – after the more archaic totem – of the father, whom his oedipal beasty-boys are destined to kill.[41]

4

The Number of Beasts

The third famous case, in which the analysis of unconscious material leads Freud from animality to infantile sexuality and the Oedipus complex, is presented in his essay *From the History of an Infantile Neurosis*, written in 1914 and published in 1918. In the history of psychoanalysis, it is known as the Wolf Man case. Wolf Man was Freud's pseudonym for Sergei Pankejeff, an educated Russian aristocrat from Odessa, who, aged twenty-three, became Freud's patient in 1910. He was born in a rather happy marriage, but there were serious psychological and psychosomatic issues in his family background. After the suicide of his sister in 1906 and of his father in 1907, Pankejeff felt severely depressed and cut off from reality as if by a veil. His body suffered too: for instance, he could not even pass bowel movements without an enema, for which he needed assistance.

The psychoanalysis of the Wolf Man took longer than the treatment of any of Freud's other patients: it lasted from 1910 until 1914 when Freud imagined he was cured, while actually he was not: there were more sessions in the subsequent years. Freud was not his only therapist: before

72   The Number of Beasts

and after, he was diagnosed and treated by many doctors, including the famous psychiatrists Vladimir Bekhterev in St. Petersburg, Theodor Ziehen in Berlin, and Emil Kraepelin in Munich, as well as by psychoanalyst Ruth Mack Brunswick. Although, in defiance of Freud's claims, Pankejeff's engagement with psychoanalysis did not lead to his recovery in any conventional sense, he lived a long life and died at the age of ninety-two, having left behind remarkable memoirs and drawings.[1] From the perspective of today's positivist psychiatry, Freud's psychoanalytic therapy of Pankejeff may have been erroneous, since the patient's psychic condition should first have been stabilized not with talking, but with medication.[2] However, the Wolf Man himself preferred psychoanalysis – probably because he found it more spiritually or intellectually challenging. After all, for his rather artistic personality, the adventure of working with Freud was not so much a cure as a creative collaboration, a way of narrating his experiences, and a dangerous trip into the depths of his own soul, guided by the Virgil from Vienna. In turn, his case became the source of insights of crucial importance for the Freudian method.

What is common between the two Freudian beasty boys, the Rat Man and the Wolf Man, is that their stories fall under the psychoanalytical category of obsessional neurosis, the language of which, according to Freud, must be understood as "only a dialect of the language of hysteria."[3] While Little Hans is diagnosed with anxiety-hysteria, and the Rat Man with obsessional neurosis, the Wolf Man, according to Freud, suffers with both conditions and presents a sort of synthesis of them. His nickname refers to his wolf phobia, with which he suffered as a little child. He was also afraid of other animals, such as butterflies, beetles, and caterpillars, while at the same time being cruel to them. As Freud says of Pankejeff's early childhood:

> There was a particular picture-book, in which a wolf was represented, standing upright and striding along. Whenever he caught sight of this picture he began to scream like a

The Number of Beasts

lunatic that he was afraid of the wolf coming and eating him up. His sister, however, always succeeded in arranging so that he was obliged to see this picture, and was delighted at his terror. Meanwhile he was also frightened at other animals as well, big and little. . . . Yet he could also remember that at this very time he used to torment beetles and cut caterpillars to pieces. Horses, too, gave him an uncanny feeling. If a horse was beaten he began to scream, and he was once obliged to leave a circus on that account. On other occasions he himself enjoyed beating horses.[4]

Prior to having these symptoms, Pankejeff's parents observed a drastic alteration in his character: from being "a very good-natured, tractable, and even quiet child" to being "disconnected, irritable and violent."[5] They ascribed this change to an effect on him of an English governess whom they had hired to look after him, and who turned out to be a quarrelsome person, addicted to drink, unlike his old nurse (Nanya), an uneducated country woman, to whom the boy was very attached (in noble Russian families, nurses were much closer to children than their mothers). The new governess was soon sent away, but the boy's character did not improve.

Another trait of the little Wolf Man's personality, intensely discussed in connection with his illness, is his piety of which Freud says: "He related how during a long period he was very pious. Before he went to sleep he was obliged to pray for a long time and to make an endless series of signs of the cross. In the evening, too, he used to make the round of all the holy pictures that hung in the room, taking a chair with him, upon which he climbed, and used to kiss each one of them devoutly."[6] Just as his fear of animals paradoxically coincides with cruelty towards them, his piety is coupled with fits of blasphemy, such as repeating thought associations "God-swine" or "God-shit," as well as superstitions and compulsive rituals. When he sees someone for whom he feels sorry – like poor, old, or disabled people, for instance – he has to breathe out noisily so as not to become like them[7] – as if

74   The Number of Beasts

there was a risk that he might inhale their condition as an infection. In Russian, the word "breath" has the same root as "spirit": he breathes in the Holy Ghosts and breathes out the evil spirits: this is the meaning of the ritual, which, after seeing his father in a sanatorium, Pankejeff supposedly began to practice at the age of six. Plagued by severe depression, his father looked ill and miserable, the "prototype of all the cripples, beggars, and poor people in whose presence he was obliged to breathe out."[8] At the same time, Freud notes, the ritual of breathing out reveals the boy's strong identification with his father as if trying to exhale him as a kind of disease with which he could have been infected or as the evil spirit, or demon, by which he was possessed. Another significant person with whom the Wolf Man unconsciously identifies is his sister, in whose image compulsive breathing out merges with the strange association: "God-swine." These two symptoms are connected for the Wolf Man through the biblical legend of exorcising demons: "When he heard that Christ had once cast out some evil spirits into a herd of swine which then rushed down a precipice," Freud reports, "he thought of how his sister in the earliest years of her childhood, before he could remember, had rolled down on to the beach from the cliff-path above the harbour. She too was an evil spirit and a swine."[9]

The chain of events is mixed up in the patient's memory, and he tends to present as simultaneous what was sequential. Meanwhile, as Freud's analysis suggests, the state of piety and superstition, the excessive manifestations of which reveal obvious symptoms of obsessional neurosis, *replaces* his early anxiety-hysteria in the form of animal phobia rather than coincides with it. Little Wolf Man begins his psychic journey from phobia, which he then gets rid of, but only at the cost of moving on to another disorder. His flight from fear of animals to the obsession with God occurs after his mother and Nanya indoctrinate him into Christianity and read him the Bible. According to Freud, he does not simply turn to religion, but makes

The Number of Beasts 75

a passage from one religious system to another, namely, from totemism with its focus on animals as gods and ancestors, to Christian monotheism. To be more precise, his shift is not from one religion to another but from one mental state to another, which, in Freud's perspective, correspond to these religious systems. What is at stake in both cases is a certain configuration of the machine of masculinity presented by Freud as the Oedipal complex, with the central figure of the father, who comes either in the guise of a totem animal, like a scary wolf from the children's book, or like God-father, who sent his human son to suffer and die on the cross: "In his wolf phobia he had gone through the stage of the totemic father-surrogate; but that stage was now broken off, and, as a result of new relations between him and his father, was replaced by a phase of religious piety."[10]

What triggers the state of anxiety, which first crystallizes in the fear of the wolf, and then in the fear of God? Freud argues that the basic mechanism of the Wolf Man's disorder is similar to other cases of anxiety-hysteria: at its origin, there is a libido, which undergoes repression, converts into fear and then becomes attached to animals which happen to be around. This is the case with Little Hans, who projected his fear onto the horses he regularly observed. This is also the case with the Wolf Man, whose fear chooses as its object wolves featuring in children's books and Russian lullabies. "A grey wolf will come at night, and will take of you a bite": even nowadays, every Russian knows this song by heart; we hear it from our mothers, and we sing it to our children. The same motif from one generation to another: paradoxically, it is supposed to quieten us. As an adult, I still cover myself with a duvet in such a way that no piece of my body remains open enough to lure the wolf. Of course, I know that he will never come; I am in Berlin, on the tenth floor of a new apartment building, and there are no wolves around – only rare foxes in the neighborhood. But in the archives of my body, this script for the theater of the soul is recorded in my mother tongue and filed in the memory of my people. But if a psychoanalyst happened to witness my body wrapped up in a duvet, wouldn't she catch by the tail a sexual wolf from which I am trying to protect myself? In other words, is there some infantile libido beyond this fear? Freud would say yes. It is deeply forgotten, as if buried in memory – recorded, but also re-coded beyond all recognition.

In Freud's interpretation, the libidinal background of little Wolf Man's fear is the "inverted Oedipus complex"[11]: what makes him so unhappy and unwell is an unconscious incestuous fantasy, the content of which is not sexual contact with his mother but desire for his father. Freud's analysis reveals three essential components of this desire: masochism (a fantasy of being beaten by his father), cannibalism (a fear of being eaten by the father/wolf), and homosexuality. The last component, according to Freud, creates the Wolf Man's core psychic conflict: a fantasy of being sexually abused by his father together with his masculinity actively protesting against this fantasy that remains censored. It can only reach consciousness through the mediation of mental disorders that smuggle it in under the guise of fear of wolves, and then in the guise of excessive piety.

This is where my first question arises: if, according to Freud, what stands behind anxiety is a sexual fantasy, then what stands behind the sexual fantasy? From a real trauma of sexual abuse, implied by Freud's original seduction theory, the answer shifts, in his book *Totem and Taboo*, to a mythic phylogenetic heritage, i.e., the murder by brothers of the alpha-male of a primitive horde as prequel to the drama of Oedipality. It might seem that, by refuting his seduction theory, shifting his emphasis from reality to fantasy, and thereby reconciling his theory of the origins of hysteria with the common sense of his time, Freud takes a step back. However, looking more closely at these two options, we can find that they are not so antagonistic, in so far as the phylogenetic theory implies a trauma, albeit not an individual trauma, rather the reconstruction of a generic, ancestral trauma as individual fantasy. After all,

The Number of Beasts 77

fantasy and reality are not merely opposite to each other. There is a dialectical relation between them, in which sexuality seems to operate as a third term. Both traumatic seduction and the murder of the ancestral father (the totem animal) are hypotheses outlined by Freud with the aim "to establish the foundations of incest prohibition in reality,"[12] even if this reality refers to immemorial mythic times. Whereas the fantasy theory pointed to the religious foundations of little Wolf Man's early libidinal experiences, the trauma theory would suggest that he had actually been abused.[13] If that were the case, then, in (mis)taking reality for fantasy, Freud displayed a sort of myopia, but, paradoxically, he was still on the right track. The hidden content of a fantasy revealed in the course of analysis may very well point to actual facts or have similar pathogenic consequences: even if the boy wasn't abused, he was still abused in so far as his fantasy reenacted some mythic theater of cruelty, fancifully rearranged by the baby Eros as the theater of desire, wherein he could appear as a she, a woman with whom he identified, his sister, his mother, or just a girl like me, like you.

Suggesting that the little Wolf Man as a child was seduced by his sister, while on a somewhat deeper level having masochistic fantasies about his father, Freud in his account of this patient does not only balance hypotheses about trauma and fantasy. He also arrives at a third hypothesis in which these two are combined: the hypothesis of the primal scene (*Urszene*). This third hypothesis involves postulating the child's observation or fantasy of watching sexual intercourse between two parents, observed or fantasized by a little child, who is unaware of its meaning and might understand it as a scene of violence. This scene, according to Freud, triggers both psychic trauma and physical excitement: without knowing about sexuality, the child nevertheless appears to be able to prefigure its experiences. As I already mentioned, together with the hypothesis of seduction and the myth of the murder of the father of the primitive horde, this theory blurs the line between reality

78   The Number of Beasts

and fantasy, and represents the most speculative, meta-physical side of Freud's enterprise.

What leads Freud to his theory of the primal scene is his interpretation of the nightmare that Pankejeff recalls having on the eve of his fourth birthday. The nightmare, which incidentally might have triggered his animal phobia, comes as the culmination of his psychoanalytic treatment by Freud and provides the clue to the Wolf Man's psychic theater. Pankejeff recalls it as follows:

> I dreamt that it was night and that I was lying in my bed. (My bed stood with its foot towards the window; in front of the window there was a row of old walnut trees. I know it was winter when I had the dream, and night-time.) Suddenly the window opened of its own accord, and I was terrified to see that some white wolves were sitting on the big walnut tree in front of the window. There were six or seven of them. The wolves were quite white, and looked more like foxes or sheep-dogs, for they had big tails like foxes and they had their ears pricked like dogs when they pay atten-tion to something. In great terror, evidently of being eaten up by the wolves, I screamed and woke up.[14]

You wonder how, from this child's nightmare, Freud arrives at the idea – highly improbable as it seems – that the baby must have been traumatized by happening to witness his parent's sexual intercourse? In Freud's psycho-analysis, there are no direct but only roundabout ways. Following the flow of associations, we must proceed from the manifest to the latent content of the dream. So the analysis begins with wolves. Usually they are grey, and never climb trees. Their strange appearance in Pankejeff's dream is telling, but what does it tell us? What do the wolves mean? Freud asks more concrete questions: Why are they white? How did they come to be on the tree? How many are they? He goes through these questions in detail, and provides the patient's associations with his sexualized interpretations of them, the main motif of which is, obvi-ously, the fear of the father represented by the wolf.

The Number of Beasts   79

According to Freud, the white color of the wolves alludes to large flocks of sheep, which the boy, together with his father, used to see in the neighborhood of their estate. The position of the wolves sitting in the tree refers to the story, told him by his grandfather, about a tailor who once caught a wolf by his tail and pulled it off, and then met a pack of wolves in the forest: in fear, the tailor climbed up a tree, but the wolves stood one upon another in order to reach him. (In Freud's perspective, the imagery of wolves' tails – be they cut off or replaced with fancy white bushy fox tales – signifies fear of castration.) Elements of folklore are of great importance, because what anchors Pankejeff's psychic theater is not only his family story, but also a general European cultural tradition, into which he is drawn through narratives. If we are to stick to Freud's idea that the little Wolf Man is on a psychic trip from totemism to Christian monotheism, then the narrative that corresponds to the later monotheist stage of his illness (obsessional neurosis) is definitely the Bible, while the earlier totemic phase (animal phobia) is fostered by fairy tales, most notable those featuring wolves, such as "Little Red Riding Hood" and "The Wolf and the Seven Little Goats." The latter is intensely discussed by Freud with regards to the question of the number of wolves.

Pankejeff made several drawings of his dream, but he could not remember how many wolves were sitting in the tree – seven, six, or even five? Freud finds an interesting explanation of this uncertainty. No doubt the patient heard from his nanny a Brothers Grimm fairy tale "The Wolf and the Seven Little Goats." In this story, a mother-goat leaves her seven kids alone and goes off for milk. While she is gone the wolf gets into the house. The kid-goats have time to hide in different places, but the wolf finds them anyway and eats them. Only one of the goats manages to survive. He hides in the wall clock, from where he watches the scene of the wolf devouring his sisters and brothers. "Here the number seven occurs, and also the number six, for the wolf only ate up six of the little goats, while the

80 The Number of Beasts

seventh hid itself in the clock-case,"[15] comments Freud. The seventh kid-goat is blurred, because he escaped. He is not part of the scene, but a witness to it. And this little survivor can be identified as the dreamer himself. From his safe space he observes a group of kid-goats, his siblings, now turned into strange wolves (as if they were bitten by a werewolf). Within Freud's interpretative frame, this material reveals that infantile fear of the father is amplified by the motif of cannibalism, which could have originated, for instance, from the acts of "affectionate abuse" shared by his father with many other adult people in relation to their children: "it is possible that during the patient's earlier years his father (though he grew severe later on) may more than once, as he caressed the little boy or played with him, have threatened in fun to 'gobble him up.'"[16]

During one of his psychoanalytic appointments, the Wolf Man shares a powerful insight with Freud. He notes that all wolves in the dream are motionless. The only movement in this dream is made by his bedroom window that suddenly opens before his eyes. The Wolf Man interprets this as meaning: "My eyes suddenly opened."[17] The function of the eyes in the dream is symbolically delegated to the window. Think about this transposition: your eyes are the window that protects the bedroom of your body from the outside world, but they also open themselves up to this world. The window of the eyes opens, just like the stage curtain in the theater opens – and you see a scene. A wolf theater. The wolves perform motionlessly. They are staring at you. Who or what do they play? We might already think about the kid-goats, eaten by the wolf – and they themselves look like wolves because the wolf who ate them is their father. The one who survived – the Wolf Man – looks at them through the open eyes of his room as if from the clock-case. But this is not the whole story.

According to Freud, one of the basic principles of the formation of dreams and therefore of their interpretation is reversal: any content can be interpreted as the opposite to how it appears. In the case of the wolves looking at the

The Number of Beasts

boy, "the distortion would consist in an interchange of subject and object, of activity and passivity: being looked at instead of looking."[18] Therefore, the subject of the gaze must be the boy himself, as if looking with wolf's eyes at something in the place where he is supposed to be. As Freud observes: "The attentive looking, which in the dream was ascribed to the wolves, should rather be shifted on to him."[19] I am wrapping myself up in my blanket in fear of the wolf that will come from the outside. But the wolf is inside.

The window placed between the eyes of the boy and the eyes of the wolves operates as a mirror. This metaphor will be amplified by Jacques Lacan, in whose interpretation the reversal of the fascination of the gaze between the boy and the wolves constitutes "the navel of the dream" and refers to a "privileged experience" of the encounter of the subject with its own ultimate innermost truth which is at the same time an absolute alterity: "What's at issue is an essential alien [dissemblable], who is neither the supplement, nor the complement of the fellow being [semblable], who is the very image of dislocation, of the essential tearing apart of the subject. The subject passes beyond this glass in which he always sees, entangled, his own image."[20] Thus Lacan puts the interpretation of the Wolf Man's dream into a peculiar dialectical frame: what happens there is not merely a symbolic reversal, but a structural passage of opposites: the inner self of the subject comes from the Other. We never really coincide with ourselves: at the beginning, there is always a rupture, a gap, and no identity is possible without the rough work of difference. What psychoanalysis calls "unconscious" and we call "soul" is an alien, a stranger.

This dialectical solution will gain another dimension, if we translate it into the language of cultural anthropology. It is a large field of research, indeed, and I do not pretend to exhaust the scope of interpretative possibilities. I will only make one reference to the all-time classics, which I find the most literal. In his book *Golden Bough*, James G. Frazer discusses the motif in folklore of the so-called

The Number of Beasts

"external soul." He refers to a number of fairy tales in which wizards, witches, and other similar characters are endowed with the power to remove souls from bodies and put them into animals, plants, or inanimate objects such as boxes and jars. As long as these receptacles are secured, the bodies that are bound to them stay alive and safe as well. Frazer connects this imagery to the system of totemism. A group of people – a tribe, a clan – binds itself to a particular animal or plant, calls themselves by its name and worships it, because their life is literally stored in this external being.[21] Note that the totem might also be praised as an ancestor of the group, as a forefather, but also that the totem animal can be sacrificed. This brings us back to Freud's own version of anthropology, grounded in the myth of the killing of the father of the prehistoric horde. The totem as the external soul of the people refers to the traumatic potential of ancestry which Freud defines as phylogenetic inheritance: it is as if the totem mediated between the lives of individuals and the memory of the genus. That is: between the living and the dead.

Let me call the eye-to-eye contact between the boy and the wolves – which drags him down into mental illness – *the totemic moment.* It is his own terrifying ancestral self that appears at the stage of the wolf theater. But what exactly does the boy, now played by the group of wolves, see at the place where, according to the dream's disposition, he must be located himself? What is he scared of? The structure of the scene becomes more complex as we understand that the image of the wolves is not just the mirror in which the boy would only see his own gaze. There is a sort of parallax vision that reveals something else behind the scene: something that is seen by the boy – who is seen by the wolves – but that is different from wolves. "*Something terrible,*" says Freud.[22] The logic of reversal allows him to skip the complexity of these optical effects: "instead of immobility (the wolves sat there motionless; they looked at him, but did not move) the meaning would have to be: the most violent motion. That is to say, he suddenly woke

The Number of Beasts   *83*

up, and saw in front of him a scene of violent movement at which he looked with strained attention."[23]

With this interpretative gesture, the wolves retreat, and the stage is set for another scene. What follows is preempted by Freud's signature remark: "I have now reached the point at which I must abandon the support I have hitherto had from the course of the analysis. I am afraid it will also be the point at which the reader's belief will abandon me."[24] Our belief is supposed to vanish right after Freud shares his hypothesis of the primal scene: behind the nightmare of the wolves hides a traumatic content – an act of his parents having sex, observed by the boy in his very early childhood. Freud argues that this episode took place when Pankejeff was about one-and-a-half years old:

> He was suffering at the time from malaria, an attack of which used to come on every day at a particular hour. . . . Probably for the very reason of this illness, he was in his parents' bedroom. . . . When he woke up, he witnessed a coitus *a tergo* [from behind], three times repeated; he was able to see his mother's genitals as well as his father's organ; and he understood the process as well as its significance.[25]

The Wolf Man strongly objected to this interpretation, which he found "terribly far-fetched."[26] At least, in Russian aristocratic families, it was not customary for children to sleep in their parents' rooms; and even if he did fall really ill, he would stay close to his nanny, who was looking after him.[27] Freud, however, did not seem to care much for the probability of his hypothesis. There is neither evidence that what he presented as an outcome of his analysis happened for real, nor even traces of such a fantasy in the patient's recollections. The primal scene is a speculative concept. As noted by Lacan, its specificity is that it is not revealed, but logically (re)constructed: "Nothing emerges in the memory of the subject – we will have to ask ourselves about this term memory – which might lead to talking about the resurrection of the scene, but everything forces one to the conviction that it did indeed happen in this way."[28]

84 The Number of Beasts

Indeed, Freud's conclusion has become the target of irony and criticism. One of the most famous passages along these lines belongs to Gilles Deleuze and Felix Guattari. In the second chapter of their *Thousand Plateaus*, "1914: One or Several Wolves?", they argue that Freud's analysis is wrong in that it reduces the wilderness of the child's psyche to the all-too-human family story. Insisting that what really matters are not the boy's parents, but the wolves themselves, Deleuze and Guattari address them as an affective animal multiplicity, and summarize the sequence of Freudian arguments for the primal scene as follows:

> We witness Freud's reductive glee; we literally see multiplicity leave the wolves to take the shape of goats that have absolutely nothing to do with the story. Seven wolves that are only kid-goats. Six wolves: the seventh goat (the Wolf-Man himself) is hiding in the clock. Five wolves: he may have seen his parents make love at five o'clock, and the roman numeral V is associated with the erotic spreading of a woman's legs. Three wolves: the parents may have made love three times. Two wolves: the first coupling the child may have seen was the two parents *more ferarum*, or perhaps even two dogs. One wolf: the wolf is the father, as we all knew from the start. Zero wolves: he lost his tail, he is not just a castrater but also castrated. Who is Freud trying to fool? The wolves never had a chance to get away and save their pack: it was already decided from the very beginning that animals could serve only to represent coitus between parents, or, conversely, be represented by coitus between parents.[29]

This summary is quite precise. Notably, it focuses on counting the beasts and showing how their number becomes fewer and fewer with each new interpretative step. Deleuze and Guattari focus on the question of the number of wolves because in their own interpretation the Wolf Man is not a neurotic, but a schizoid personality, who has multiple selves. Wolves always travel in packs, they say – everybody knows this, even a little child knows this, only Freud does not. The unconscious is "fundamentally a crowd," which

The Number of Beasts 85

he mistakes for a single person.[30] According to Deleuze and Guattari, the attentive gaze of the wolves must be read as a silent call to join their pack – to which the little Wolf Man might have belonged in the first place. He is invited to become a part of them, to become-wolf. This brings us back to the totemic moment: an encounter with the animal other, which constitutes the navel of Pankejeff's dream, displays the "external soul." What if the group of five, sex or seven wolves were ambassadors delegated by his ancestral crowd to deliver the invitation? In the context of totemism, his ancestral crowd would mean: his people. Not Russians or something just as human. Wolves. I am peeking out from under my blanket: outside the window, in the night flashes a multiplicity of yellow eyes.

As a single individual, you cannot really join the pack. Becoming-wolf is a schizoid experience of psychic multiplicity: "you can't be one wolf, you're always eight or nine, six or seven. Not six or seven wolves all by yourself all at once, but one wolf among others, with five or six others."[31] We are in a composition of wolves, always immediately the entire pack, together with the others, among their number. And it is this irreducible multiplicity, that, according to Deleuze and Guattari, Freud substitutes with the unity of the Oedipal narrative, step by step (re)constructing an identity of a normal person out of the schizoid animal pack. In Freud's interpretation of the Wolf Man case, the uncountable wolves are replaced first by domestic and farm animals – goats, sheep, and sheep-dogs – and then by human beings – the heteronormative parental couple. In contrast to this, Deleuze and Guattari are fascinated by the wilderness of the wolf pack, and show no concern for either humans or goats.

I would like, however, to look at the vortex of transformations involving wolves, goats, humans, and other animals, as well as to attempts to count them, from yet another angle. This will enable us to pay justice to intermediate actors like goats, and to reveal an important role that they play in this story. Human beings transform into animals, and animals of various species into each other: those are magical transformations that are encrypted into different folklore traditions. The material provided by fairy tales is genuinely queer, and introduces narratives on diverse experiences of becoming, to which children are extremely receptive. The wolves' delegates can invite the boy to join their pack for a magic trip where he is supposed to lose himself, but perhaps find something new instead. But are they really wolves? Dissatisfied with Freud's suggestion that these are just the boy's parents in the guise of wolves, we should not, however, put too much trust in their own wolf-ness, praised by Deleuze and Guattari. Look at those wolves. With their white color and their bushy foxy tails, they are always already on the way to some other form of life, and if in the next moment they appear as goats, this can mean that in this particular ontological region a goat can do what a wolf cannot (in Morocco, for instance, goats climb trees).

Taking a step back to the beginning of the analysis will help us to clarify this moment. As was already mentioned, Freud addressed the change in character that happened to the little Wolf Man – from the early animal phobia to religious piety, that is, from anxiety-hysteria to the obsessional neurosis – as a shift from the totemic to the Christian phase of his illness. Accordingly, there was a change in the boy's reading list – from animal fairy tales to the Holy Bible. Freud referred to a particular story from the *New Testament*, which seemed to contribute to the formation of major symptoms of his obsessional neurosis, such as his loud breathing out on seeing the sick or the poor – the legend of the exorcism of the Gerasene demoniac. Let me recall what that was about.

According to the Gospel of Mark, Jesus and his disciples were traveling by sea. When they arrived in the region of the Gerasenes (in other versions – Gadarenes or Gergesenes), they found a man who was possessed by some unclean spirit, wore no clothes, and dwelled not in a house but around tombs: "And always, night and day,

The Number of Beasts 87

in the tombs and in the mountains, he was crying out, and cutting himself with stones." When Jesus asked what his name was, the demon replied: "My name is Legion: for we are many." There was a herd of swine, feeding nearby on the mountainside. So, Jesus commanded the legion of demons to come out of the man and to enter the swine, which then rushed down and drowned in the sea.[32]

This is a miracle: the demons withdraw, and the man is left alone, healed. Now he can remember his own name, go back home, return to his family, and (re)socialize with fellow humans. Together with the legion of evil spirits that tormented him from inside, the animal multiplicity, embodied in the herd of swine, retreats and gives way to the integrity of the human person. In other words, he is cured. At least, this is what we think has happened to him in the absence of being provided with evidence about his later life and further experiences. Jesus cured him of what was later called madness, and then mental illness. Translated into the language of today's psychiatry, possession might be classified among the symptoms of dissociative disorder, hysteria, psychosis, schizophrenia, or other mental illnesses. The herd of swine drowning in the sea is an exteriorized madness, an insanity in its, so to say, objective form. An external wounded soul stored in these particular animal bodies.

I don't think that the healing of the Gerasene demoniac had anything to do with the rituals of exorcism, which, in some places, are still performed by Christian priests. What if in reality, in order to bring the sufferer to his senses, Jesus just talked to this person, asked him what his name was and so on, and treated him as a human being? And conversely, what if the talking cure of psychoanalysis is a form of exorcism? From this perspective, the transformation of the wolves from Pankejeff's dream into the goats from Grimm's fairy tale and then into his own parents, which Deleuze and Guattari call a reduction, looks like a miracle of the analysis. It is as if Freud would literally send the uncountable pack of demonic wolves, by which

88   The Number of Beasts

the patient was possessed, into the herd of goats (somewhat similar to the herd of pigs feeding nearby) in order to make both the wolves and the goats disappear. There is a nuance, however: when Pankejeff comes to Freud, wolves only exist as a memory, and not as an actual symptom. It is as if it was Jesus himself who already chased those wolves away. I mean, the totemic "possession," which Freud diagnoses as anxiety-hysteria and Deleuze and Guattari attribute to schizophrenia, seems to disappear with the boy's conversion to Christianity. Yet the mental transformation that happens to him, when he switches from fairy tales to the Bible, is not a cure, but a passage from possession to obsession.

Adhering to Freudian anthropo-theological insight about the Wolf Man's passage from totemism to Christianity, I think of it in the context of a broader history of religion, and particularly in the context of the way animals gradually lose their superior sacred status with the advent of monotheisms and the banishing of the remnants of more ancient systems of beliefs. In Christianity, the animals that might have been totems for archaic communities, reappear as demons. Their positive social agency is forgotten, or, to be more precise, it is repressed. Notably, demons are called unclean spirits and associated with unclean animals, such as swine, in whose bodies the Gerasene demons find their last refuge, or such as goats that are often related to the cult of Satan. The division of animals into clean and unclean is older than Christianity, but it also belongs to the Biblical tradition. According to the Book of Leviticus, clean animals are those that can be eaten or sacrificed, and unclean are those that cannot. It is the God of the Old Testament who puts animals at human disposal and subjugates them to human needs.

Another legend is instructive in this regard – the story of Noah's Ark, told in the Old Testament Book of Genesis (5–8). Angry at people for the sins they had committed, God decided to destroy the world and to wipe everything off the face of the Earth. In order to give humanity

The Number of Beasts 89

another chance, he commissioned a righteous man named Noah to build an ark big enough to accommodate Noah himself, his family, and the representatives of all animal species.

The orders that God gives to Noah with regards to the number of beasts are quite specific: "And of every living thing of all flesh, two of every sort shalt thou bring into the ark, to keep them alive with thee; they shall be male and female. Of fowls after their kind, and of cattle after their kind, of every creeping thing of the earth after his kind; two of every sort shall come unto thee, to keep them alive."[33] Then follows another, updated instruction: "Of every clean beast thou shalt take to thee by sevens, the male and his female: and of beasts that are not clean by two, the male and his female. Of fowls also of the air by sevens, the male and the female; to keep seed alive upon the face of all the earth."[34]

It is absolutely clear that all animals are rescued in pairs in order to be able to reproduce. Why then are clean animals taken in by sevens? Perhaps the principle of selection was obvious for the people of the Old Testament, and made good practical sense. Given that clean animals are those that can be eaten or sacrificed, besides each one couple meant to reproduce its species, two extra couples might have been taken on board as a food supply. But seven is an odd number. One member of each group of seven would have been single, with no mate: a sacrificial animal. Thus, only a limited number of animals will survive during the flood. Imagine animals from everywhere in the world – from the North, East, South, and West – going all the way to Noah's land; a crowd of animals, queuing around the ark, perhaps in panic, stressed, and disoriented. Only one couple or seven of each species is allowed to get on board. Which one of the many? Maybe the one that Noah will consider the best, the healthiest, or the most beautiful. Or maybe they will be chosen by lot, or just picked up haphazardly. The lucky ones. All the rest will perish in the waters of the flood.

You think you will be among those who survive: at the entrance, you will show the right papers; the security staff of the last evacuation transports will let you in, say to the next one in line: "Sorry, we already have enough of your species," and close the gate. Those rejected will be left outside. From the safe space on the boat, you will watch the Legion drown: "for we are many." Now imagine that there is another group of seven that tries to get on the ark. The door is closed, but they knock at your bedroom's window at night. Wolves, but not really: strange color, strange tales, sitting in the tree. In a word, demons. In the next moment, they are goats. You say: goats are not clean animals, therefore there can be only two goats, not seven. Freud replies: yes, in fact they are two, and they are not even goats, but two unclean parents, having sex in front of their baby who suffers from malaria – and they are already right here, in this room, in the darkness of your eyes.

But let us keep counting goats, for they turn out to be very special animals. Although they are considered unclean, goats can be eaten. At least, they are eaten by wolves: this is what we learn from Grimm's fairy tale. But they can also be sacrificed. Thus, the Book of Leviticus describes an ancient Judaic ritual that took place once a year, on the holy day of Yom Kippur. The priest of Israel had to take two goats, chosen by lots. One of them was meant to be offered to God as blood sacrifice, the other to be sent away into the wilderness. Both goats embodied all the sins committed by the people throughout the year. The one sent away into the wilderness would take with him all these sins as his burden. He was called a scapegoat and associated with Azazel, the demon of the desert. Similar rituals existed in other archaic cultures. They still widely exist as spontaneous social practices not officially recognized as scapegoating: people unite against arbitrarily selected individuals or groups, which they blame for all kinds of negative experiences. Notably, the scapegoat itself is innocent: we have too much guilt to put on its burden; there is no room for its own sins.

According to Rene Girard, whose philosophical anthropology is based on analysis of this phenomenon, it is rooted in a universal mechanism of canalizing violence, which allows human societies to restrain aggression of all against all and mitigate the escalation of social conflict. What constantly provokes such escalation, in Girard's view, is a mimetic structure of desire, which fills our lives with jealousy and revenge. Violence generates violence, and mutual aggression draws everybody into a vicious circle, but there is a solution: instead of hating each other, we find someone, who embodies all that we count as evil. According to Girard: "any community that has fallen prey to violence or has been stricken by some overwhelming catastrophe hurls itself blindly into the search for a scapegoat."[35] Widespread violence is thus redirected against one individual, whom we blame and whom we enthusiastically punish, banish, exorcise, or destroy. Scapegoating is an unconscious mechanism that unites communities and allows its members to abuse their victims with impunity while representing the practices of collective violence as morally justified. This mechanism, according to Girard, creates a kind of anthropological invariant, which is the basis for the system of sacrifice, and the truth of which is only revealed by Christianity.

Note that in the Christian tradition Jesus, who dies for the sins of humanity, is compared to the first, slain goat of Yom Kippur, while Barabbas, who was nailed to the cross next to Jesus, but then released, is compared to the scapegoat banished to the desert. In Girard's philosophy, the figure of the scapegoat stands for a broader concept of surrogate victim. The story of Jesus reveals the truth of victim-blaming: rather than a real criminal, an innocent person who calls for love, peace and non-violence, becomes the object of the most brutal execution. What he embodies is not the demonic evil, but the goodness of God, of whom he is the son. According to Girard, Jesus becomes an ultimate scapegoat who is sacrificed for all our sins – past, present, and future. His death is our salvation; this

92   The Number of Beasts

must be the last sacrifice that would overturn the scapegoat mechanism once and for all, and put an end to the archaic tradition of sacrificial violence. All shall be redeemed by forgiveness, not vengeance.

Among the miracles performed by Jesus during his lifetime, the healing of the Gerasene demoniac carries a similar meaning: to put an end to the ongoing violence. As Girard puts it, the possessed man is "a prisoner of his own madness," but, in a sense, he is freer than others – he can live outside the city, in the wilderness, and wear no clothes. He is not bound by social convention: this is what his countrymen might already find quite irritating. His mental illness is interrupted by the "periods of remission, during which the sick man returns to the city." When a crisis is approaching, he rushes back to his "voluntary exile" in the tombs, but the people of Gerasene do not want to let him out, and bind him with chains.[36]

Girard suggests that there is a sort of "cyclical pathology" in the relation of the wretched man and his community, for which he becomes a scapegoat. Why is he cutting himself with stones? Because others were stoning him. In the tombs, he is trying to find refuge from the community, which repeatedly commits violence against him:

> They must gain some enjoyment from this drama and even feel the need of it since they beg Jesus to leave immediately and stop interfering in their affairs. Their request is paradoxical, given that Jesus had just succeeded, without any violence, in obtaining the result which they had professed to be aiming at with their chains and fetters but which, in reality, they did not want at all: the complete cure of the possessed man.[37]

According to Girard, the meaning of "Jesus' therapeutic success"[38] is precisely this: to put an end to the vicious circle of violence. Apparently, this is not what the Gerasenes want: "The inhabitants demand Jesus' departure. And Jesus gives them that satisfaction without saying a word.

The man he has cured wants to follow him, but he urges him to remain with his own people."[39]

Another legendary character addressed by Girard and particularly important in the context of my Freudian meditations is Oedipus. He was accused of serious crimes such as incest and parricide, blamed for causing plague in Thebes, and expelled from the city. We should not forget, however, that initially, when he was an infant, his father Laius doomed him to death by having him abandoned in the desert. Adhering to Marie Delcourt's hypothesis that this involved offering little Oedipus as a scapegoat, Girard comments: "The murder by exposure of weak or ill-formed infants was extremely widespread and is certainly associated with the concept of the surrogate victim – that is, with the unanimous basis of all sacrificial rites."[40] Notwithstanding, this act of preemptive paternal violence involving infanticide remains shielded by the parricidal guilt of Oedipus.

Let me go back to the group of the wolf-like kid-goats on a tree outside the Wolf Man's bedroom window. As Freud explained, in terms of a fairy tale told by the Brothers Grimm, the seventh wolf-like kid-goat – the Wolf Man himself – hides in the clock-case, while the others are eaten by the wolf. But, as we just figured out, he is also the scapegoat meant to be sacrificed. Notably, Pankejeff is identified with all three legendary surrogate victims addressed by Girard: the Gerasene demoniac, Jesus, and Oedipus. His possession by the pack of demons-wolves is released in a totemic moment of his anxiety-hysteria. His obsession corresponds to the neurotic phase of pious identification with Jesus who chases away the demons, but who is sent to his death by his God-father. Finally, he is obsessed with his father, from whom, in Freud's argument, the little inverted Oedipus unconsciously desires to receive a similar punishment.

As for the other goats, they might have all been eaten by the wolf, and now they themselves look like wolves. Freud explains that the real wolf is the boy's father, whom he

94 The Number of Beasts

fears (but behind fear, there is an inverted Oedipal desire). This wolf is lurking as a strange father-mother, who might eat the goats in order to make them reappear from his belly as wolves (another fairy tale, addressed in the analysis, "Little Red Riding Hood" has this trope: at the end, the bad wolf is caught, his belly cut open, and those who have been eaten by him are released). The Wolf Man's recollection of a book illustration with which his sister used to scare him in childhood plays a significant role – it depicts a wolf standing on its hind legs and reaching out a forelimb. Note the extraordinary position of this wolf, uncharacteristic of its species.

For Deleuze and Guattari, the wolf is not an individual set of properties but rather one of the names for the intensity of affect. Although wolves always travel in packs, there is still room left for a lone wolf. He runs alongside and at the same time a bit apart from his pack. He can be a leader or an outcast. Deleuze and Guattari call such an animal an exceptional individual, demon, or anomaly. They define this as "a phenomenon of bordering." The anomaly's body creates a borderline of the pack, beyond which "the multiplicity changes nature."[41] It borders between different multiplicities, which Deleuze and Guattari generically define as packs. Of course, they are aware of the fact that animal multiplicities organize themselves in complex ways, depending on their species, not only as packs, but also as herds, flocks, swarms, colonies, and so on. A pack or a band for Deleuze and Guattari is not a characteristic, but a mode in which an encounter between animal and human being occurs.[42]

I would like, however, to make a distinction between two animal multiplicities that are at stake here, and of which Deleuze and Guattari only privilege one: a pack of wolves and a herd of goats with a monstrous human-like figure of the father-wolf bordering between them and producing the pack of wolves from the herd of goats that he devours (the devoured goats become wolves). The difference between the herd and the pack is the difference

The Number of Beasts   95

between the devoured and the devouring. These are not just characteristics, but two different existential and affective modes. The wolf is involved in both, on the one hand as a father of the goat family, on the other hand as a representative of his own wolf pack. An interesting perspective on this ambiguity is proposed by Jacques Derrida, who, at the beginning of his seminar about the sovereign and the beast, puts together a fantastic series of different cultural representations of wolves. This series points to the domain of political philosophy. It departs from Rousseau's critical remark made in the *Social Contract* about Hobbes and Grotius who see "the human race divided into herds of cattle, each one with its chief who keeps it in order to devour it."[43] The chief of the cattle is precisely the wolf of which Derrida says:

> [H]e, the chief, does not keep the beast by devouring it, while devouring the beast (and we are already in the space of *Totem and Taboo* and the scenes of devouring cruelty that are unleashed in it, put down, repressed in it and therefore displaced in it into symptoms; and the devouring wolf is not far away, the big bad wolf, the wolf's mouth, the big teeth of Little Red Riding Hood's Grandmother-Wolf ("Grandmother, what big teeth you have"), as well as the devouring wolf in the *Rig Veda*, etc., or Kronos appearing with the face of Anubis devouring time itself).[44]

Kronos is one of classical Greece's supreme gods, ancient personification of time. He devours his children when they are still infants, because he fears that one of them is destined to kill him. In the end, of course, this is what happens: Kronos eats five of his infants (according to the myth they are Hestia, Demeter, Hera, Hades, and Poseidon); the sixth infant, Zeus, manages to survive (his mother Rhea goes to Crete and gives birth to him in a cave, slipping Kronos a stone in his place); Zeus overthrows (and in some versions castrates) his father and releases from his belly the other devoured children. Thus, we have five devoured children, the sixth who survived (hidden in a cave). If

96 The Number of Beasts

we are speaking of a different version of the same story, then there should be a seventh child. Who is he? Kronos himself. This is how we can interpret Derrida's mysterious phrase "Kronos appearing with the face of Anubis devouring time itself." He, the wolf, is the one of us, just like the leader, who takes care of our herd in order to devour it in due course. Among other wolves, he is sitting in the tree in Pankejeff's dream. A wolf in white sheep clothes. You either kill him or become him. In this latter case, you have first to be eaten by him, but there is a way to avoid this: by finding a scapegoat, chasing a rat, beating a horse – that is, by passing a symbolic threshold beyond which some kind of violence is the norm.

We hardly notice when we cross that threshold, and here we have frightened boys growing fluffy tails and making important decisions – about the future of the world, about preventive attacks, about who should live and who should die. Such is our patriarchal machine at work. In times of war, when the state turns to openly devouring its sons, it becomes visible, as in the following poem by Velimir Khlebnikov, written in the wake of the First World War:

> "Hey!" the wolf cries out in blood,
> "I eat the meat of strong young men!"
> and a mother says: "My sons are gone."
> But we are your elders! *We* decide![45]

And what about sex? We almost forgot about it insofar as the bloody scene of devouring replaced the Oedipal eroticism of the primal scene. However, one more final nuance of counting goat-wolves allows us to locate the fantasy of love right within the scene of violence. As I mentioned with regards to Noah's ark, among each group of seven animals one single individual was meant to be sacrificed, and two couples eaten. But there was one more couple of each species – actually, the first one – that was taken to reproduce and continue life on Earth. Here comes my new version of the scene. Five wolves: one kid-goat is to be

The Number of Beasts

sacrificed (but he is hiding in the clock-case), four others are to be eaten. The two remaining animals from the seven undertake the task of reproduction: they are the parental couple. Eventually, their coupling performance is observed by the boy from his hiding place. It is "a matter of indifference," says Freud, "whether we choose to regard it as a primal *scene* or as a primal *phantasy*."[46] What matters, however, is the origin of this scene, which Freud locates in the memory of our species.

In the closing paragraphs of his analysis of the Wolf Man case, Freud reflects upon the existence of a "hereditary, phylogenetically acquired factor in mental life" and introduces the idea that, somehow, little children – and he means really little babies – might have some knowledge, comparable to an animal instinct, from the very moment of their birth: "If human beings too possessed an instinctive endowment such as this, it would not be surprising that it should be very particularly concerned with the processes of sexual life, even though it could not be by any means confined to them."[47] What does this mean? That sexuality is not something that we learn from experience, but something that we inherit, and this "phylogenetically inherited schemata," which in Freud's psychoanalysis appear as "primal fantasies," has the quality of knowledge. They are like innate ideas, which Plato in *Phaedo* presented as proof of the immortality of the soul: we knew them even before being born. It is as if our souls brought this material into life from the kingdom of the dead, where they resided before entering our bodies.

Freud's account of sexuality is a materialist version of the immortality of the soul, in which the symbolic kingdom of the dead is indicated as a sort of collective memory, to which we are attached through unconscious fantasies. These fantasies repeat – or rehearse – the same scripts again and again: a vicious circle of normalization of patriarchal practices of violence, infanticide as a preventive action justified by fantasies of parricide, excessive animal cruelty to which we turn a blind eye each and every day, the culture of abuse and victim-blaming, scapegoating, and war. All the three Freudian cases, addressed above – Little Hans, the Rat Man, and the Wolf Man – unfold as a series of scenes that are staged for the theater of our psyche as erotic, but there seems to be nothing erotic going on backstage. An anthropological mechanism of the production of the social and psychic norm sucks us into its wheels, and sexuality comes as a sort of additive that converts pain into pleasure. Refusing it – staying with the animal, with a horse that is being beaten, a rat that is being chased, a wolf that is being trapped, a scapegoat, and, eventually, with crucified God – might lead to a Nietzschean madness, a refusal, conscious or not, to be a part of humanity. But the good news is that systemic, preemptive, devouring violence of fathers that takes place on backstage of sexual performance is still not the ultimate reality. Behind the scene of desire, or, as Freud would say, destiny, there is not only violence, but love that connects us with others at some basic, animalistic level. The experiences of childhood with its psychic diversity and incredible openness toward multispecies love might reveal an impressive archive of alternative scenarios outside of the machine of masculinity and its erotic supplements. The plan is indeed ephemeral, but that's the way it is: find your animals, be kind to them, learn to forgive, and step by step discover the magic of becoming a girl.

Notes

Introduction

1 See, on this, my essay: Oxana Timofeeva, *Это не то* [*This Is Not That*] (Saint Petersburg: Ivan Limbakh Publishing House, 2022), 68–93.

2 The article under my name can still be found in the printed version of the journal: Oxana Timofeeva, Крысиная нора: Фрейд, Фуко и проблема изоляции [Rathole: Freud, Foucault and the Problem of Isolation], *Logos*, vol. 2 (2021): 1–28. A short version was published here: Oxana Timofeeva, "Rathole: Beyond the Rituals of Handwashing" (*e-flux*, no. 119 (June 2021): https://www.e-flux.com/journal/119/400227/rathole-beyond-the-rituals-of-handwashing/)

The Theatre of the Soul

1 See the original post: https://www.facebook.com/nastya.melny chenko/posts/10209108320800151

2 Sigmund Freud and Josef Breuer, *The Standard Edition of the Complete Psychological Works of Sigmund Freud, Vol. II* (London: The Hogarth Press, 1955), 30.

3 ὕστερα – uterus, womb (Greek).

4 Paul Verhaeghe, *Does the Woman Exist? From Freud's Hysteric to Lacan's Feminine* (New York: Other Press, 1999), 17.

100 Notes to pp. 9–19

5 *The Standard Edition, Vol. II*, 6.
6 Ibid., 7.
7 Verhaeghe, *Does the Woman Exist?*, 9.
8 *The Standard Edition, Vol. II*, 125.
9 Ibid., 127.
10 Ibid., 130.
11 Ibid., 133.
12 Ibid., 134.
13 Alenka Zupančič, *The Odd One In: On Comedy* (Cambridge, MA: MIT Press), 171.
14 Peter Gay, *Freud – A Life for Our Time* (New York: W.W. Norton & Company, 2006), 93.
15 Ibid., 94.
16 *The Standard Edition of the Complete Psychological Works of Sigmund Freud, Vol. XXII* (London: The Hogarth Press, 1964), 120.
17 *The Standard Edition of the Complete Psychological Works of Sigmund Freud, Vol. XVI* (London: The Hogarth Press, 1963), 368.
18 Ibid., 369.
19 Ibid., 370.
20 https://www.netall.ru/society/news/1103569.html
21 *The Standard Edition of the Complete Psychological Works of Sigmund Freud, Vol. VII* (London: The Hogarth Press, 1953), 173–203.
22 *The Standard Edition of the Complete Psychological Works of Sigmund Freud, Vol. XIII* (London: The Hogarth Press, 1955), 1–162.
23 Octave Mannoni, *Freud* (New York: Vintage Books, 1974), 121.
24 *The Standard Edition, Vol. XVI*, 370–1.
25 Cf. Jeffrey M. Masson, *The Assault on Truth: Freud's Suppression of the Seduction Theory* (New York: Ballantine Books, 2003).
26 Sándor Ferenczi, "Confusion of Tongues Between Adults and the Child – The Language of Tenderness and of Passion," *Contemporary Psychoanalysis*, vol. 24, no. 2 (1988): 196–206, 201.
27 See on this: *The Standard Edition of the Complete Psychological Works of Sigmund Freud, Vol. XVIII* (London: The Hogarth Press, 1955), 12–43.
28 Rebecca Comay, *Mourning Sickness: Hegel and the French Revolution* (Stanford, CA: Stanford University Press, 2011), 148.

A Horse Is Being Beaten

1 "Widdler" in English translation.
2 *The Standard Edition of the Complete Psychological Works of Sigmund Freud, Vol. X* (London: The Hogarth Press, 1955), 21.
3 See, for example, his interpretation of the boy's dream about giraffes: "The big giraffe is myself, or rather my big penis (the long neck)" (*The Standard Edition, Vol. X*, 38).
4 See on this: Jerome C. Wakefield, "Concept Representation in the Child: What Did Little Hans Mean by 'Widdler'?" *Psychoanalytic Psychology*, vol. 34, no. 3 (2017): 352–60.
5 *The Standard Edition, Vol. X*, 30.
6 "I: 'Used you often to play at horses?' *Hans:* 'Very often. Fritzl was the horse once, too, and Franzl the coachman; and Fritzl ran ever so fast and all at once he hit his foot on a stone and bled" (*The Standard Edition, Vol. X*, 58).
7 In the original German text "Seelischen," from "Seele" (soul).
8 *The Standard Edition, Vol. X*, 115.
9 Ibid., 116.
10 Ibid., 25.
11 Ibid., 22.
12 Ibid., 46.
13 Ibid.
14 In all quoted dialogues between Hans and his father, the first person is the father, Max Graf.
15 Ibid., 49–50.
16 Ibid., 50.
17 Ibid., 125.
18 Ibid.
19 Ibid., 136.
20 Ibid., 136–7.
21 Ibid., 125.
22 "Hans did not dispute this interpretation; and a little while later he played a game consisting of biting his father, and so showed that he accepted the theory of his having identified his father with the horse he was afraid of" (ibid.).
23 Ibid., 79.
24 Ibid.
25 Ibid.
26 Vladimir Mayakovsky, "Kindness to Horses." https://ruverses.com/vladimir-mayakovsky/good-treatment-of-horses/3544/
27 *The Standard Edition, Vol. X*, 58.

102 Notes to pp. 30–39

28 Milan Kundera, *The Unbearable Lightness of Being* (New York: Harper & Row, 1984), 290.
29 *The Standard Edition, Vol. X*, 79.
30 Ibid., 80.
31 Ibid., 81.
32 Ibid., 52.
33 Ibid., 88–9.
34 Ibid., 94.
35 See Slavoj Žižek, *Violence* (New York: Picador, 2008), 58–73.
36 "Berlin's Wonderful Horse; He Can Do Almost Everything but Talk – How He Was Taught," *The New York Times*, September 4, 1904. https://timesmachine.nytimes.com/timesmachine/1904/09/04/101396572.pdf
37 Ibid.
38 "'Clever Hans' Again. Expert Commission Decides That the Horse Actually Reasons," *The New York Times*, October 2, 1904. https://timesmachine.nytimes.com/timesmachine/1904/10/02/120289067.pdf
39 Oskar Pfungst, *Clever Hans (The Horse of Mr. von Osten): A Contribution to Experimental Animal and Human Psychology* (New York: Henry Holt, 1911).
40 Kevin Roose, "Bing's A.I. Chat: 'I Want to Be Alive,'" *The New York Times*, February 16. 2023. https://www.nytimes.com/2023/02/16/technology/bing-chatbot-transcript.html
41 *The Standard Edition, Vol. X*, 97.
42 *The Standard Edition of the Complete Psychological Works of Sigmund Freud, Vol. XXI* (London: The Hogarth Press, 1961), 183.
43 *The Standard Edition of the Complete Psychological Works of Sigmund Freud, Vol. XVII* (London: The Hogarth Press, 1955), 175–204.
44 Serge Leclaire, *A Child Is Being Killed* (Stanford, CA: Stanford University Press, 1998), 5–6.
45 Brian Massumi, *Ontopower: War, Powers, and the State of Perception* (Durham, NC: Duke University Press, 2015), vii.
46 Thus, in 2022, Russian president Vladimir Putin justified the military attack on Ukraine by saying that otherwise Ukraine would have attacked Russia.
47 Leclaire, *A Child Is Being Killed*, 6.
48 "For in our opinion the Oedipus complex is the actual nucleus of neuroses, and the infantile sexuality which culminates in this complex is the true determinant of neuroses" (*The Standard Edition, Vol. XVII*, 193).
49 *The Standard Edition, Vol. XXI*, 179.

50 Ibid., 181.
51 Ibid.
52 Ibid., 182.
53 Ibid., 183.
54 Ibid.
55 Ibid., 186.
56 Ibid., 177.
57 Ibid., 196.
58 Fyodor Dostoevsky, *Crime and Punishment* (The Project Gutenberg EBook, 2006). https://www.gutenberg.org/cache/epub/2554/pg2554-images.html
59 Ibid.
60 Ibid.
61 Nikolai K. Mikhailovsky, *Dostoevsky – A Cruel Talent* (Ann Arbor, MI: Ardis, 1978), 11.
62 Dostoevsky, *Crime and Punishment*.
63 See Michael John Di Santo, "'Dramas of Fallen Horses': Conrad, Dostoevsky, and Nietzsche," *Conradiana*, vol. 42, no. 3 (2010): 45–68, 48; Fyodor Dostoevsky, *The Notebooks for Crime and Punishment* (Chicago, IL: University of Chicago Press, 1967), 64; Fyodor Dostoevsky, *A Writer's Diary, Volume One: 1873–1877* (Evanston, IL: Northwestern University Press, 1997), 328–9.
64 Valery Podoroga, *Mimesis: Analytic Anthropology of Literature. Vol. 1: N. Gogol, F. Dostoevsky* (Moscow: Cultural Revolution; Logos-Altera, 2006), 449.
65 Ibid., 449–50.
66 *The Standard Edition, Vol. X*, 146.
67 Dostoevsky, *Crime and Punishment*.
68 Vladimir Putin, Nataliya Gevorkyan, Natalya Timakova and Andrei Kolesnikov, *First Person: An Astonishingly Frank Self-Portrait by Russia's President Vladimir Putin* (PublicAffairs, 2000), 10.
69 Ibid., 10.
70 Rebekah Koffler, "How Putin's Rat-Infested Childhood Shaped His Philosophy on War," *New York Post*, March 12, 2022, https://nypost.com/2022/03/12/how-putins-rat-infested-childhood-shaped-his-philosophy-on-war/; Uri Friedman, "Vladimir Putin and the Parable of the 'Cornered Rat,'" *The Atlantic*, August 2, 2023, https://www.theatlantic.com/international/archive/2023/08/putin-russia-ukraine-war-cornered-rat-story/674890/

104 Notes to pp. 50–63

The Rathole

1 *The Standard Edition, Vol. X*, 158.
2 Ibid., 199.
3 Ibid., 205.
4 Ibid., 206.
5 Ibid.
6 Peter Gay (Ed.), *The Freud Reader* (New York: W.W. Norton & Company, 1989), 310.
7 *The Standard Edition, Vol. X*, 213.
8 Ibid., 215–16.
9 Ibid., 215.
10 Ibid., 195–6.
11 Ibid., 197.
12 Ibid., 198.
13 *The Standard Edition of the Complete Psychological Works of Sigmund Freud, Vol. XX* (London: The Hogarth Press, 1959), 122.
14 Ibid.
15 Michel Foucault, "Security, Territory, Population," *Lectures at the Collège de France, 1977–1978* (London: Palgrave Macmillan, 2007), 25.
16 Michel Foucault, *History of Madness* (London: Routledge, 2006), 5.
17 Michel Foucault, *Discipline and Punish: The Birth of the Prison* (New York: Vintage Books, 1995), 195.
18 Ibid.
19 Ibid., 196.
20 Ibid., 198.
21 Ibid., 199.
22 Ibid.
23 Friedrich Nietzsche, *The Complete Works. Vol. VIII. Beyond Good and Evil. On the Genealogy of Morality* (Stanford, CA: Stanford University Press, 2014), 246–85.
24 Foucault, *Discipline and Punish*, 249.
25 Ibid., 195.
26 Cf: Elisabeth S. Linde, Tibor V. Varga and Ami Clotworthy, "Obsessive-Compulsive Disorder during the COVID-19 Pandemic: A Systematic Review," *Front Psychiatry*, vol. 13 (2022): 806872.
27 Emma Russell, "OCD: I spent 20 years preparing for the coronavirus pandemic," BBC, May 10, 2020. https://www.bbc.com/news/stories-52564434

Notes to pp. 65–72 105

28 See Mannoni, *Freud*, 168; Jacques Lacan, *Écrits: The First Complete Edition in English* (New York: W.W. Norton & Company, 1999), 336.
29 Maarten 't Hart, "Rats," *Granta* (July 2004), https://granta.com/rats/
30 Alexander Pogrebnyak cited this episode in his paper presented at the conference "Catastrophe and Utopia" at Stasis Center for Practical Philosophy at the European University at St. Petersburg, June 15, 2020.
31 Cf. Henri Legrand Du Saulle, *La folie du doute (avec délire du toucher)* (Paris: Adrien Delahaye, 1875).
32 Foucault, *History of Madness*, 45–6.
33 Rene Descartes, *The Philosophical Writings of Descartes, Volumes 1–2* (Cambridge: Cambridge University Press, 1985), 13
34 Foucault, *History of Madness*, 47.
35 Michel Serres, *The Parasite* (Baltimore, MD: Johns Hopkins University Press, 1982), 12.
36 Nina Savchenkova, "O razume, utrativshem tselesoobraznost, paraliche voli i pornographii" ["On reason that lost its reasonability, paralysis of will, and pornography," Sigmund Freud, *Sobranie Sochinenij v 26 tomakh [Complete works in 26 volumes]*, Vol. 4 (St. Petersburg, 2007), 281.
37 Byung-Chul Han, *The Agony of Eros* (Cambridge, MA: MIT Press, 2017), 4.
38 G.W.F. Hegel, *Lectures on the History of Philosophy, in 3 volumes. Vol. III. Medieval and Modern Philosophy* (Lincoln, NE: University of Nebraska Press, 1985), 217.
39 Ibid., 250–1.
40 Ibid., 252.
41 *The Standard Edition, Vol. XVII*, 114.

The Number of Beasts

1 Sigmund Freud, *The Wolf Man and Sigmund Freud*, edited by Muriel Gardiner (New York: Basic Books, 1972).
2 Cf.: "There is no question that today the Wolf Man would be diagnosed as having a bipolar affective disorder with psychotic features. It is doubtful that Freud was aware of this, as he focused exclusively on the psychodynamic origins of the Wolf Man's depressions. Kraepelin, in contrast, would have likely diagnosed the Wolf Man accurately as manic-depressive, as he diagnosed the father... Today, the Wolf Man would have likely

106 Notes to pp. 72–83

been started on lithium carbonate or other mood-stabilizing medication and treated prophylactically between mood episodes" (Mark L. Ruffalo, "Freud's Wolf Man in the Era of Modern Psychiatry," *Psychology Today*, July 2019, https://www.psychologytoday.com/us/blog/freud-fluoxetine/201907/freuds-wolf-man-in-the-era-modern-psychiatry).

3 *The Standard Edition, Vol. X,* 157.
4 *The Standard Edition, Vol. XVII,* 16.
5 Ibid., 15.
6 Ibid., 16.
7 Ibid., 17.
8 Ibid., 67.
9 Ibid.
10 Ibid., 114.
11 Ibid., 119.
12 Mannoni, *Freud,* 132.
13 Thus, with reference to Ruth Mack Brunswick's unpublished paper, Arnold Rachman argues that Freud's patient was abused by someone from the family. See Arnold W.M. Rachman, *Psychoanalysis and Society's Neglect of the Sexual Abuse of Children, Youth, and Adults: Re-Addressing of Freud's Original Theory of Sexual Abuse and Trauma* (London: Routledge, 2022), 19.
14 *The Standard Edition, Vol. XVII,* 29.
15 Ibid., 31.
16 Ibid., 34.
17 Ibid.
18 Ibid., 35.
19 Ibid., 34.
20 *The Seminar of Jacques Lacan, Book II: The Ego in Freud's Theory and in the Technique of Psychoanalysis, 1954–1955* (New York: W.W. Norton & Company, 1991), 176–7.
21 James G. Frazer, *The Golden Bough: A Study in Magic and Religion* (London: Macmillan Press, 1922), 874–904.
22 *The Standard Edition, Vol. XVII,* 34.
23 Ibid., 35.
24 Ibid., 36.
25 Ibid., 36–7.
26 Karin Obholzer, *The Wolf-Man: Conversations with Freud's Patient – Sixty Years Later* (New York: Continuum Books, 1982), 35.
27 Daniel Goleman, "As a Therapist, Freud Fell Short, Scholars Find," *The New York Times,* March 6, 1990, https://www.

Notes to pp. 83–97 107

nytimes.com/1990/03/06/science/as-a-therapist-freud-fell-short-scholars-find.html
28 *The Seminar of Jacques Lacan, Book II*, 176.
29 Gilles Deleuze and Felix Guattari, *A Thousand Plateaus: Capitalism and Schizophrenia* (Minneapolis, MN: University of Minnesota Press, 2005), 28.
30 Ibid., 29–30.
31 Ibid., 29.
32 Mark 5:1–20.
33 Gen. 6.
34 Gen. 7.
35 Rene Girard, *Violence and the Sacred* (New York: Continuum, 2005), 84.
36 Rene Girard, *The Scapegoat* (Baltimore, MD: Johns Hopkins University Press, 1986), 168.
37 Ibid., 169.
38 Ibid., 175.
39 Ibid., 164.
40 Girard, *Violence*, 122; Cf. Marie Delcourt, *Légendes et cultes de héros en Grèce* (Paris, 1942), 102.
41 Deleuze and Guattari, *A Thousand Plateaus*, 245.
42 Ibid., 239.
43 Jean-Jacques Rousseau, *Du contrat social* (Paris: Classiques Garnier, 1954), 237, cited in: Jacques Derrida, *The Beast and the Sovereign, Vol. 1* (Chicago, IL: University of Chicago Press, 2009), 11–12.
44 Derrida, *The Beast and the Sovereign*, 12.
45 Velimir Khlebnikov, *Collected Works. Vol. II. Prose, Plays and Supersagas* (Cambridge, MA: Harvard University Press, 1989), 311.
46 *The Standard Edition, Vol. XVII*, 120.
47 Ibid.

Bibliography

"Berlin's Wonderful Horse; He Can Do Almost Everything but Talk – How He Was Taught," *The New York Times*, September 4, 1904. https://timesmachine.nytimes.com/timesmachine/1904/09/04/101396572.pdf

"'Clever Hans' Again. Expert Commission Decides That the Horse Actually Reasons," *The New York Times*, October 2, 1904. https://timesmachine.nytimes.com/timesmachine/1904/10/02/120289067.pdf

Comay, Rebecca, *Mourning Sickness: Hegel and the French Revolution* (Stanford, CA: Stanford University Press, 2011).

Delcourt, Marie, *Légendes et cultes de héros en Grèce* (Paris, 1942).

Deleuze, Gilles and Felix Guattari, *A Thousand Plateaus: Capitalism and Schizophrenia* (Minneapolis, MN: University of Minnesota Press, 2005).

Derrida, Jacques, *The Beast and the Sovereign, Vol. 1* (Chicago, IL: University of Chicago Press, 2009).

Descartes, Rene, *The Philosophical Writings of Descartes, Volumes 1–2* (Cambridge: Cambridge University Press, 1985).

Di Santo, Michael John, "'Dramas of Fallen Horses': Conrad, Dostoevsky, and Nietzsche," *Conradiana*, vol. 42, no. 3 (2010): 45–68.

Dostoevsky, Fyodor, *A Writer's Diary, Volume One: 1873–1877* (Evanston, IL: Northwestern University Press, 1997).

Bibliography 109

Dostoevsky, Fyodor, *Crime and Punishment* (The Project Gutenberg EBook, 2006). https://www.gutenberg.org/cache/epub/2554/pg2554-images.html

Dostoevsky, Fyodor, *The Notebooks for Crime and Punishment* (Chicago, IL: University of Chicago Press, 1967).

Du Saulle, Henri Legrand, *La folie du doute (avec délire du toucher)* (Paris: Adrien Delahaye, 1875).

Ferenczi, Sándor, "Confusion of Tongues Between Adults and the Child – The Language of Tenderness and of Passion," *Contemporary Psychoanalysis*, vol. 24, no. 2 (1988): 196–206.

Foucault, Michel, *Discipline and Punish: The Birth of the Prison* (New York: Vintage Books, 1995).

Foucault, Michel, *History of Madness* (London: Routledge, 2006).

Foucault, Michel, "Security, Territory, Population," *Lectures at the Collège de France, 1977–1978* (London: Palgrave Macmillan, 2007).

Frazer, James G., *The Golden Bough: A Study in Magic and Religion* (London: Macmillan Press, 1922).

Freud, Sigmund, *The Standard Edition of the Complete Psychological Works, Vol. II*, with Josef Breuer (London: The Hogarth Press, 1955).

Freud, Sigmund, *The Standard Edition of the Complete Psychological Works, Vol. VII* (London: The Hogarth Press, 1953).

Freud, Sigmund, *The Standard Edition of the Complete Psychological Works, Vol. X* (London: The Hogarth Press, 1955).

Freud, Sigmund, *The Standard Edition of the Complete Psychological Works, Vol. XIII* (London: The Hogarth Press, 1955).

Freud, Sigmund, *The Standard Edition of the Complete Psychological Works, Vol. XVI* (London: The Hogarth Press, 1963).

Freud, Sigmund, *The Standard Edition of the Complete Psychological Works, Vol. XVII* (London: The Hogarth Press, 1955).

Freud, Sigmund, *The Standard Edition of the Complete Psychological Works, Vol. XVIII* (London: The Hogarth Press, 1955).

Freud, Sigmund, *The Standard Edition of the Complete Psychological Works, Vol. XX* (London: The Hogarth Press, 1959).

Freud, Sigmund, *The Standard Edition of the Complete Psychological Works, Vol. XXI* (London: The Hogarth Press, 1961).

Freud, Sigmund, *The Standard Edition of the Complete Psychological Works, Vol. XXII* (London: The Hogarth Press, 1964).

Freud, Sigmund, *The Wolf Man and Sigmund Freud*, edited by Muriel Gardiner (New York: Basic Books, 1972).

110 Bibliography

Friedman, Uri, "Vladimir Putin and the Parable of the 'Cornered Rat,'" *The Atlantic*, August 2, 2023, https://www.theatlantic.com/international/archive/2023/08/putin-russia-ukraine-war-cornered-rat-story/674890/

Gay, Peter, *Freud – A Life for Our Time* (New York: W.W. Norton & Company, 2006).

Gay, Peter (Ed.), *The Freud Reader* (New York: W.W. Norton & Company, 1989).

Girard, Rene, *The Scapegoat* (Baltimore, MD: Johns Hopkins University Press, 1986).

Girard, Rene, *Violence and the Sacred* (New York: Continuum, 2005).

Goleman, Daniel, "As a Therapist, Freud Fell Short, Scholars Find," *The New York Times*, March 6, 1990, https://www.nytimes.com/1990/03/06/science/as-a-therapist-freud-fell-short-scholars-find.html

Han, Byung-Chul, *The Agony of Eros* (Cambridge, MA: MIT Press, 2017).

Hart, Maarten 't, "Rats," *Granta* (July 2004), https://granta.com/rats/

Hegel, G.W.F., *Lectures on the History of Philosophy, in 3 volumes. Vol. III. Medieval and Modern Philosophy* (Lincoln, NE: University of Nebraska Press, 1985).

Khlebnikov, Velimir, *Collected Works. Vol. II. Prose, Plays and Supersagas* (Cambridge, MA: Harvard University Press, 1989).

Koffler, Rebekah, "How Putin's Rat-Infested Childhood Shaped His Philosophy on War," *New York Post*, March 12, 2022, https://nypost.com/2022/03/12/how-putins-rat-infested-childhood-shaped-his-philosophy-on-war/

Kundera, Milan, *The Unbearable Lightness of Being* (New York: Harper & Row, 1984).

Lacan, Jacques, *Écrits: The First Complete Edition in English* (New York, W.W. Norton & Company, 1999).

Lacan, Jacques, *The Seminar of Jacques Lacan, Book II: The Ego in Freud's Theory and in the Technique of Psychoanalysis, 1954–1955* (New York: W.W. Norton & Company, 1991).

Leclaire, Serge, *A Child Is Being Killed* (Stanford, CA: Stanford University Press, 1998).

Linde, Elisabeth S., Tibor V. Varga and Amy Clotworthy, "Obsessive-Compulsive Disorder during the COVID-19 Pandemic: A Systematic Review," *Front Psychiatry*, vol. 13 (2022). 10.3389/fpsyt.2022.806872

Mannoni, Octave, *Freud* (New York: Vintage Books, 1974).

Bibliography

Masson, Jeffrey M., *The Assault on Truth: Freud's Suppression of the Seduction Theory* (New York: Ballantine Books, 2003).

Massumi, Brian, *Ontopower: War, Powers, and the State of Perception* (Durham, NC: Duke University Press, 2015).

Mayakovsky, Vladimir, "Kindness to Horses," https://ruverses.com/vladimir-mayakovsky/good-treatment-of-horses/3544/

Mikhailovsky, Nikolai K., *Dostoevsky – A Cruel Talent* (Ann Arbor, MI: Ardis, 1978)

Nietzsche, Friedrich, *The Complete Works. Vol. VIII. Beyond Good and Evil. On the Genealogy of Morality* (Stanford, CA: Stanford University Press, 2014).

Obholzer, Karin, *The Wolf-Man: Conversations with Freud's Patient – Sixty Years Later* (New York: Continuum Books, 1982).

Pfungst, Oskar, *Clever Hans (The Horse of Mr. von Osten): A Contribution to Experimental Animal and Human Psychology* (New York: Henry Holt, 1911).

Podoroga, Valery, *Mimesis: Analytic Anthropology of Literature. Vol. 1: N. Gogol, F. Dostoevsky* (Moscow: Cultural Revolution; Logos-Altera, 2006).

Putin, Vladimir, Nataliya Gevorkyan, Natalya Timakova and Andrei Kolesnikov, *First Person: An Astonishingly Frank Self-Portrait by Russia's President Vladimir Putin* (PublicAffairs, 2000).

Rachman, Arnold W.M., *Psychoanalysis and Society's Neglect of the Sexual Abuse of Children, Youth, and Adults: Re-Addressing of Freud's Original Theory of Sexual Abuse and Trauma* (London: Routledge, 2022).

Roose, Kevin, "Bing's A.I. Chat: 'I Want to Be Alive,'" *The New York Times*, February 16. 2023. https://www.nytimes.com/2023/02/16/technology/bing-chatbot-transcript.html

Rousseau, Jean-Jacques, *Du contrat social* (Paris: Classiques Garnier, 1954).

Ruffalo, Mark L., "Freud's Wolf Man in the Era of Modern Psychiatry," *Psychology Today*, July 2019, https://www.psychologytoday.com/us/blog/freud-fluoxetine/201907/freuds-wolf-man-in-the-era-modern-psychiatry

Russell, Emma, "OCD: I spent 20 years preparing for the coronavirus pandemic," *BBC*, May 10, 2020. https://www.bbc.com/news/stories-52564434

Savchenkova, Nina, "O razume, utrativshem tselesoobraznost, paraliche voli i pornographii" ["On reason that lost its reasonability, paralysis of will, and pornography," Sigmund Freud, *Sobranie Sochinenij v 26 tomakh [Complete works in 26 volumes]*, Vol. 4 (St. Petersburg, 2007).

Bibliography

Serres, Michel, *The Parasite* (Baltimore, MD: Johns Hopkins University Press, 1982).

Verhaeghe, Paul, *Does the Woman Exist? From Freud's Hysteric to Lacan's Feminine* (New York: Other Press, 1999).

Wakefield, Jerome C., "Concept Representation in the Child: What Did Little Hans Mean by 'Widdler'?" *Psychoanalytic Psychology*, vol. 34, no. 3 (2017): 352–60.

Žižek, Slavoj, *Violence* (New York: Picador, 2008).

Zupančič, Alenka, *The Odd One In: On Comedy* (Cambridge, MA: MIT Press).

Index

alienation
  and isolation 68
  Rat Man case 52, 68
amnesia
  and hysteria 54–5, 63
  infantile 15
animal cruelty 54, 97
  Little Hans case 28, 46
  Rat Man case 52, 54, 65, 68
animal phobia 2
  and Wolf Man 74, 78, 79,
    86
animal soul 2, 29, 67
animal(s) 20, 29
  and Clever Hans effect 34
  division of into clean and
    unclean 88
  intelligence 34
  losing of superior sacred
    status 88
  in male gender socialization 1
  and Noah's Ark 89
  sacrifice 16, 82, 88
  totem 16

totemic moment 5
  see also horses; rats; wolves
Anna O case 8–9
anthropogenesis 17
anthropology 5
  cultural 17, 81–2
  Freud's version of 82
  philosophical 2, 17, 45
  psychoanalytic 35
anxiety-hysteria 24–5
  and Little Hans 24–7, 72
  and Wolf Man 74, 88, 93
artificial intelligence 34–5

Barabbas 91
beasts 2, 71–98
Bekhterev, Vladimir 72
Bentham, Jeremy 60
Bible
  and Wolf Man 2, 79, 86, 88
Bing 34
Book of Leviticus 88, 90
Brothers Grimm 79, 93
Brunswick, Ruth Mack 72

114   Index

Burke, Tarana 7
Bush, George W. 37

cannibalism 16
  and Wolf Man case 76, 80
Cartesianism *see* Descartes,
  René
castration, fear of 16
  and Little Hans 23, 25, 31,
    36
  Wolf Man case 79
ChatGPT 34
children
  infantile memories as
    products of imagination
    13–14
  killing of by father 36–7
  sexual abuse of 10
Christianity 37, 91
  and Wolf Man 74, 75, 79,
    86, 88
  see also Bible
Clever Hans effect 34
Clever Hans (horse) 33–4, 35
clinical psychology 1
Comay, Rebecca 19
COVID-19 pandemic 3, 61–2
  and obsessional neurosis
    63–4
  and OCD 62–3
  and self-isolation 61, 62
cultural anthropology 17, 81–2

Darwin, Charles, *On the Origin
  of Species* 33
death drive 19
Delcourt, Marie 93
Deleuze, Gilles and Guattari,
  Felix 84–5, 88, 94
  Thousand Plateaus 84
demons
  association with unclean
    animals 88
  exorcism of 2, 74, 86–7

Gerasene demoniac 86–7, 88,
  92–3
depression, and OCD 68
Derrida, Jacques 95, 96
Descartes, René 66–70
  and animals 68
  and doubt 66–9
  and obsessional neurosis 68
  and reason 70
  and unity of soul and body
    69–70
desire 70, 98
  destiny as 38, 98
  and Oedipus myth 38
destiny 98
  as desire 38
  and Little Hans 35
  and Oedipus myth 38
Di Santo, Michael John 45
disciplinary control/power 57,
  58–9, 61–2, 63, 67
  and COVID-19 pandemic 61
  and Foucault 57, 58–60
  and isolation 60–1
  and Nietzsche 60
  passage to self-control from
    60
  and plague city 59–60, 63
  and sovereign exclusion
    59–60, 67
Dostoevsky, Fyodor 35, 38–46
  childhood and family
    background 39
  Crime and Punishment 41–5,
    46
  epilepsy and hysteria 38–9
  and machine of masculinity
    45–6
  and Oedipus complex 40, 41
  parallels between Little Hans
    and Raskolnikov character
    40–1, 46–7
  preoccupation with cruelty
    and torture 43

Index

psychological insights 41
violence in literature of 45
doubt
Cartesian 66–9
and Freud 69
of love 68
and madness 66–7, 68
and obsessional neurosis 66–7
dreams 80–1
see also Wolf Man case

education 46–7
ego 56
epidemics 57–8
epilepsy 38–9
Eros 6, 56
exclusion 61–2
sovereign *see* sovereign exclusion
exorcism 86–7
of demons 2, 74, 86–7
talking cure as form of 87
"external soul" 82, 85

fairy tales 86
and Frazer's *Golden Bough* 82
and Wolf Man 79, 88, 90, 93
fantasy(ies)(phantasies) 3, 18
infantile 12–15, 16–17
origin of 16–17
primal 16–17, 97
and reality 76–8
unconscious 12, 17
and Wolf Man 77
fathers, as abusers 10–11, 12
Ferenczi, Sándor 18, 65
"Confusion of tongues between adults and the child" 18
Foucault, Michel 4, 57–61, 63, 66–7
Discipline and Punish 58, 59

History of Madness 58
Madness and Civilization 58
Security, Territory, Population 57
Frazer, James G., *Golden Bough* 81–2
Freud, Sigmund
Analysis of a Phobia in a Five-Year-Old Boy 21–49, 50
"A Child Is Being Beaten" 4, 36
Dostoevsky and Parricide 35, 38–9
engagement with myths 15–16, 17
"The etiology of hysteria" 12, 17
"Femininity" 12
"From the History of an Infantile Neurosis" 71–98
Inhibition, Symptoms and Anxiety 56
lecture on formation of symptoms 16–17
methodology 36
Notes Upon a Case of Obsessional Neurosis 50–70
and philosophy 1–2
seduction theory and disavowal of 10–13, 17–18, 76
Studies on Hysteria 10
Three Essays on the Theory of Sexuality 15
Totem and Taboo 15, 76, 95
visit to America and "plague" quote 65
Freud, Sigmund and Breuer, Josef, *Studies on Hysteria* 8

gender socialization 22
male 1, 40

116 Index

Gerasene demoniac 86–7, 88, 92–3
German Board of Education 33
Girard, René 4, 91–3
goats 85, 86, 87, 94–5
  relation of to the cult of Satan 88
  sacrificing of 90
  and Wolf Man case 85–6, 87–8, 90, 93–4, 96
  and "The Wolf and the Seven Little Goats" 79–80, 87, 93, 96–7
  see also scapegoat(ing)
God
  and Descartes 68, 69–70
  Freud on 70
  and Noah 88–9
  and Wolf Man 74–5
Graf, Herbert see Little Hans
Graf, Max 21, 25–8, 29, 31, 47
guilt 54
  isolation as displacement of 66
  Little Hans and fantasmatic 40
Gurevich, Vera Dmitrievna 48

Hart, Maarten 't 65
Hegel, G.W.F., Lectures on the History of Philosophy 68–70
Herzog, Werner 65
homosexuality 76
horses 5
  beating of in Dostoevsky's Crime and Punishment 41–5, 46
  beating of in the Wolf Man case 73
  in communities in 1900s 24
  exploitation and abuse of 28
  and Mayakovsky's poem 28–9

relationship between education and 33–4
witnessing of beating of by Nietzsche 29–30
see also Little Hans
hysteria 9–10, 17, 36
  and amnesia 54–5, 63
  anxiety- see anxiety-hysteria
  based on sexual trauma as a child 10–11
  derived from infantile phantasies/imagination 12–13
  and Dostoevsky's epilepsy 38–9, 40
  etiology of 10–12
  libido as cause of 24, 47
  origins and genesis 9, 10, 11–12, 76
  repetition of traumas as necessary 11
  treatment of 9
  and unconscious fantasies 17

#IAmNotAfraidToSayIt 7
incest 16, 17, 38, 77
  and Oedipus 93
infanticide 36–8
  and Oedipus myth 37–8
infantile amnesia 15
infantile phantasies 12–15, 16–17
infantile sexuality 12, 15, 17–18, 19, 24, 32, 71
  and Rat Man case 50–1, 52, 53
infection, risk of 3
inheritance, phylogenetic 16, 36, 76, 82, 97
isolation 4, 56–7, 68
  and alienation 68
  COVID-19 pandemic and self- 61, 62
  and disciplinary control 60–1

Index

as displacement of guilt 66
and economy of power 60–1
and Foucault 57–8, 60–1
and obsessional neurosis 54, 55, 56–7, 62–3, 64
and sovereign exclusion 60–1

Jesus 37, 44, 88
healing of the Gerasene demoniac 86–7, 92–3
sacrifice of 91–2
as scapegoat 91–2
Jung, Carl Gustav 65

Katharina (Aurelia Kronich) case 10–11
Khlebnikov, Velimir 96
Kraepelin, Emil 72
Krafft-Ebing, Richard von 12
Kronich, Aurelia *see* Katharina
Kronos 95–6
Kundera, Milan 29–30

Lacan, Jacques 81, 83
Laius, king of Thebes 37
Lanzer, Ernst *see* Rat Man case
Leclaire, Serge 44
A child is being killed 36–8
lepers/leprosy/leprosaria 57, 59–61
and isolation 60–1
managing of 59
and sovereign exclusion 58–9, 63
libido 47, 75
as cause of hysteria 24, 47
as love 47
Little Hans (Herbert Graf) 1, 4, 20, 21–49, 50, 98
and anxiety-hysteria 24–7, 72
beating of horses 27–8, 30, 47, 53
fear of castration 23, 25, 31, 36

fear of horses and background to 21–4, 75
and machine of masculinity 47
and Oedipus complex 22, 23, 29, 31–2, 35
parallels between Raskolnikov character and 40–1, 46–7
parents 21
psychoanalytic therapy and recovery 46–7
and theater of the soul 23–4
triggering and source of phobia of horses 25–7
and Wiwimachers 21–2, 29
"Little Red Riding Hood" 94, 95
love 98
libido as 47
mental disorder as failed 47

machine of masculinity 1, 4–5, 6
and Dostoevsky 45–6
and Little Hans 47
and Oedipus complex 46
and Wolf Man 75
madness
and doubt 66–7, 68
Foucault on 66–7
and legend of the exorcism of the Gerasene demoniac 86–7
Nietzschean 98
"madness of doubt" 66
male gender socialization 1, 40
Mannoni, Octave 16
Marx, Karl 68
masculinity, machine of *see* machine of masculinity
masochism 76
Massumi, Brian, *Ontopower* 37

118 Index

Mayakovsky, Vladimir, "Kindness to horses" 28–9
Melnychenko, Anastasia 7
#MeToo campaign 7
Mikhailovsky, Nikolay 43
myths 15–16, 17

New Testament 86–7
New York Times 33, 34–5
Nietzsche, Friedrich 29–30
  Genealogy of Morality 60
Noah's Ark 2, 88–90, 96
Nosferatu (film) 65–6
nuclear family 15

obsessional neurosis 63–4
  clinical aspects 56
  and COVID-19 pandemic 63–4
  and Descartes 68
  and doubt 66–7
  and isolation 54, 55, 56–7, 62–3, 64
  and the Rat Man case 3, 66, 72
  and taboo on touching 56
  and the Wolf Man case 72, 74, 79, 86
obsessive-compulsive disorder (OCD) 56, 64
  and COVID-19 pandemic 62–4
  and depression 68
Oedipus complex 38, 40, 71
  and Dostoevsky 40, 41
  and Little Hans 22, 23, 29, 31–2, 35
  and machine of masculinity 46
  role of parricide 35–6
  and Wolf Man 75, 76–7, 85, 94
Oedipus myth 37–8, 93
Old Testament 2, 88, 89

Pankejeff, Sergei *see* Wolf Man
Panopticon 60
Pappenheim, Bertha 8–9
parricide 15–16, 17, 33, 35–6, 37, 40, 97
penis
  absence of in women 22
  Little Hans and theory of 21–2, 25
Pfungst, Oskar 34
phantasies *see* fantasies (phantasies)
philosophical anthropology 2, 17, 45
philosophy 68–9
  and Freud 1–2
phobias
  animal *see* animal phobia
  and anxiety-hysteria 24
  horse *see* Little Hans
  origin in childhood 15
  wolf *see* Wolf Man
phylogenetic inheritance 16, 36, 76, 82, 97
plague 57, 69
  parallel between psychoanalysis and 65
  quarantine measures 59
  and rats 65
plague city 59, 61
  and disciplinary control 59–60, 63
  and isolation 61
Plato, *Phaedo* 36, 97
Podoroga, Valery 45
Pogrebnyak, Alexander 66
post-traumatic disorder 19
preemption 37
prehistoric past 16–17
primal fantasies/phantasies 16–17, 97
primal scene (*Urszene*)
  hypothesis of the 77–8

Index

and Wolf Man 77–9, 83–4, 96, 97
prisons/prisoners 57, 59
  Dostoevsky as 40
  and isolation 61
  and Panopticon 60
psychic, and the social 2, 3
psychic reality, and material reality 13–15
psychic time 11
psychic trauma 7–8, 10
  and Little Hans 27
  and repression 54–5
  theoretical discussion of sexual abuse and 8–9
  and Wolf Man 77
psychoanalysis 9, 64
  parallel between plague and 65
psychoanalytic anthropology 35
Putin, Vladimir 48
  First Person 48–9

Rat Man (Ernst Lanzer) case 3, 20, 50–70, 98
  and alienation 52, 68
  background and relationship with father 50–2
  beating of by father incident 51
  cemetery scene 53, 54, 64
  identification with the rat 53, 54
  and infantile sexuality 50–1, 52, 53
  and obsessional neurosis 3, 66, 72
  parallels with the Wolf Man 72
  rat symbolism 52
  and ratholes 52–3, 54, 64
  rats as a psychic medium 64–5

witnessing of cruelty and torture of rats 53–4
rationality, Cartesian 68
rats 5, 64–5
  and Descartes 67–8
  in *Nosferatu* 65–6
  and spread of the plague 65
  see also Rat Man case
reality, and fantasy 76–8
reason, Cartesian 70
repetition(s) 11–12, 19
repression
  and isolation 54, 55–6
  mechanisms of 54–5
Roman mythology 37
Rousseau, Jacques, *Social Contract* 95
Russia 4, 8, 48

sacrifice 44
  animal 16, 82, 88
  child 37
  goats 90
  of Jesus Christ 91–2
  and Wolf Man 93, 97
St. Petersburg 48
Saturn (Roman mythology) 37
Savchenkova, Nina 68
scapegoat/scapegoating 90–2, 96, 98
  and Jesus 91–2
  and Oedipus 93
schizophrenia 88
security 57–8, 60, 67
seduction (Freud's theory of) 10–13
  disavowal of 12, 17
  Ferenczi on 18
  and sexual abuse 10, 11, 18, 76
self-discipline 60
self-isolation 63–4
  and COVID-19 pandemic 61, 62

120   Index

Serres, Michael 67–8
sexual abuse
  and Freud's theory of
    seduction 10, 11, 18, 76
  theoretical discussion of
    psychic trauma resulting
    from 8–9
sexuality 1, 77
  and immortality of the soul
    97
  infantile *see* infantile
    sexuality
  inheritance of 97
sexualized violence 3, 7–8
  and #MeToo campaign 7
shame 3, 8
smallpox 57
soul 36, 81
  animal 2, 29, 67
  and body (Descartes) 69–70
  "external" 82, 85
  immortality of the 97
  unity of body and 69–70
sovereign exclusion 57–8, 58,
    61–2
  and COVID-19 pandemic
    61
  and disciplinary control/
    power 59–60, 67
  and isolation 60–1
  and lepers 58–9, 63
species memory 16
Spinoza 70
symbolic violence 32–3
symptoms, Freud's lecture on
    formation of 16–17

talking cure 8–9
  as form of exorcism 87
Thanatos 6, 20
theater of the soul 12, 13, 15,
    17, 23, 38, 75
Thomsen, Robert 56
totem animals 16

totemic moment 5, 82, 85, 93
totemism
  and "external soul" 82
  and Wolf Man 85
touching, taboo on 56
trauma/trauma theory 3
  and concept of infantile
    sexuality 15
  origin of as phylogenetic
    17
  and psychic time 11
  repetition of 11–12
  and Wolf Man 76–7

unconscious 70, 81, 84–5
unconscious fantasies 12, 17
unreason 67
uterus 9

Verhaeghe, Paul 9, 10
Vienna Society for Psychiatry
    and Neurology' 12
violence 1
  in Dostoevsky's literature
    45
  symbolic 32–3
von Osten, Wilhelm 33

wandering uterus 9
"war on terror" 37
Westphal, Carl 56
Wiwimacher, and Little Hans
    21–2, 29
Wolf Man (Sergei Pankejeff)
    case 1, 20, 71–98
  animal phobia 74, 78, 79,
    86
  and anxiety-hysteria 74, 88,
    93
  and Bible 2, 79, 86, 88
  and breathing out 73–4, 86
  and cannibalism 76, 80
  change from animal phobia
    to religious piety 86

Index

Deleuze and Guattari's interpretation 84–5
early childhood 72–3
family background 71
fear of and cruelty towards animals 72, 73
and Lacan 81
and legend of the exorcism of the Gerasene demoniac 86–7
and obsessional neurosis 72, 74, 79, 86
and Oedipus complex 75, 76–7, 85, 94
parallels with the Rat Man 72
and primal scene hypothesis 77–9, 83–4, 96, 97
and totemic moment 82, 85
trauma theory 76–7

white wolves nightmare 78–82, 87, 93
wolf phobia 72–3, 75
"Wolf and the Seven Little Goats" (Brothers Grimm) 79–80, 93, 96–7
wolves 5
and Deleuze and Guattari 94
and Derrida 95–6
distinction between herd of goats and pack of 94–5
and Khlebnikov's poem 96
and "Little Red Riding Hood" 94
see also Wolf Man case

Zeus 95
Ziehen, Theodor 72
Žižek, Slavoj 32
Zupančič, Alenka 11–12